YEATS
NOW

ECHOING
INTO LIFE

JOSEPH M. HASSETT

THE LILLIPUT PRESS
DUBLIN

First published 2020 by
THE LILLIPUT PRESS
62–63 Sitric Road,
Arbour Hill,
Dublin 7, Ireland
www.lilliputpress.ie

A CIP record for this publication is available
from the British Library.

10 9 8 7 6 5 4 3

Paperback ISBN 978 1 84351 778 8
Limited Edition ISBN 978 1 84351 799 3

The Lilliput Press gratefully acknowledges the financial
support of the Arts Council/An Chomhairle Ealaíon.

Designed by iota (www.iota-books.ie)
Set in 11.5 pt on 16 pt Fournier
Printed in Poland by Drukarnia Skleniarz

Contents

Introduction

Not many people think of themselves as readers of poetry. Yet when facing threshold occasions such as falling in love, marriage, the birth of a child, illness, and death, we often look for a poem to express feelings for which we don't quite seem to have the words. Why is this?

One reason is that poems can encapsulate a sentiment that cannot be grasped or expressed in any other way. John Keats alluded to this when he said that a poem 'should strike the reader as a wording of his own highest thoughts, and appear almost a remembrance'. Another is that poets are fascinated by words and spend enormous time tracking them down, pondering them, and putting them into memorable form. W.B. Yeats had an extraordinary ability to intuit the sometimes puzzling emotions that hover over recurring life experiences and to distil them into unforgettable words. His phrases seem tailored to our lives because they arose directly out of passionate moments in his own life. Believing that 'a poet's life is an experiment in living', he sought 'not to find one's art by analysis of language or amid the circumstance of dreams but to live a passionate life, and to express the emotions that find one thus in simple rhythmical language.' Robert Frost could have been describing this aspect of Yeats's work when he wrote that a poem 'ends in a clarification of life – not necessarily a great clarification, such as sects and cults are founded on, but in a momentary stay against confusion'.

Memorable Yeats lines clarify a wide range of subjects, including the meaning and comforts of friendship; the proper balance between work and life; our relationship to the universe; the intervention of a spiritual world in human life; the possibility and nature of life after death; and the role of religion in a good life. Yeats's words illuminate the path when we are pursuing or engaging with a lover; responding to hostility; finding purpose in life; searching for meaning in daily routine; growing old; suffering loss; and, inevitably, facing death. The subjects are as varied as life itself.

Many of Yeats's lines are so striking that they've taken on a life of their own and stand ready to help us express ourselves in moments of intense emotion or troubling doubt. Time and again, Yeats seems to have just the right words for the occasion. When Samuel Beckett was walking from his friend Con Leventhal's cremation, he stopped to recite lines from Yeats's 'The Tower' about death and the death of friends. The young James Joyce, lost for words at the death-bed of his fourteen-year-old brother Georgie, sang his own setting of Yeats's 'Who Goes with Fergus?'. Confronting serious illness toward the end of his life, the painter Richard Diebenkorn found creative energy in Yeats's admonition,

> An aged man is but a paltry thing,
> A tattered coat upon a stick, unless
> Soul clap its hands and sing, and louder sing
> For every tatter in its mortal dress ...

Yeats's words often have the magical air of an incantation or a spell. This is no surprise because he believed that poetry has its origins in magic. 'Have not poetry and music arisen', he asked, 'out of the sounds the enchanters made to help their imagination to enchant, to charm, to bind with a spell themselves and the passers-by?'

Yeats the enchanter is at work in his much-loved poem 'He wishes for the Cloths of Heaven'. We can hear rhythm, rhyme and repetition cast a spell in the lines describing the cloths as

> Enwrought with golden and silver light,
> The blue and the dim and the dark cloths
> Of night and light and the half-light ...

The mesmerizing sounds suggest that language has magical powers, and thus prepare the reader to accept the talismanic conclusion,

> I have spread my dreams under your feet;
> Tread softly because you tread on my dreams.

Patti Smith was enchanted by the magic of this poem when her mother read it to her at age five. She asked for a book by its author, and Yeats became an important influence on her life as a poet, songwriter, singer and memoirist.

Part of poetry's magic is that its words are linked together so skillfully that they lodge themselves in the memory, ready to be retrieved in response to a new experience. In addition, Yeats's poems were written to be spoken, and their rhetorical quality is a big part of what makes them so memorable. We can hear Yeats insisting on the importance of rhythm in a 1932 recording in which he warns, 'I'm going to read my poems with great emphasis upon their rhythm and that may seem strange if you are not used to it.' He tells of the poet William Morris raging about a public reading of one of his poems: '"It gave me a devil of a lot of trouble", said Morris, "to get that thing into verse!" It gave me', Yeats added, 'a devil of a lot of trouble to get into verse the poems that I am going to read, and that is why I will not read them as if they were prose.'

Yeats was so strongly committed to the oral performance of his poems that, after hearing a recitation by Florence Farr, he wrote, 'I have just heard a poem spoken with so delicate a sense of its rhythm, with so perfect respect for its meaning, that if I were a wise man and could persuade a few people to learn the art, I would never open a book of verses again'.

Yeats's words are meant to be listened to in both senses of the word: they are to be both heard and heeded, even when heeding opens a dialogue that ends in disagreement.

Great poets can bring coherence not only to our personal lives, but also to bewildering events in the world around us. Yeats's poems often reflect what Virginia Woolf called 'the poet's gift of turning far, abstract thoughts, if not into flesh and blood, at least into something firm and glittering'. Indeed, some of Yeats's words, such as 'the centre cannot hold' from 'The Second Coming', are quoted so often by politicians and journalists that it has been suggested that they be retired. This is a bad idea. The recurring attraction of Yeats's words is actually a testament to their magical ability to channel swirling currents of thought and emotion into memorable form. Yeats believed that the form – the style – in which ideas are expressed, quite apart from their content, can make 'us live with a deeper and swifter life'.

A sense of the magic his words could work informs Yeats's assertion that a lyric can gain 'a second beauty, passing as it were out of literature into life'. This book seeks to capture that second beauty in a compendium of words from Yeats that can help clarify and articulate our response to the world around us. The words are placed in the context of the poem, but this book focuses on the words themselves, the building blocks of poetry. To be sure, reading the complete poem will convey more of Yeats's ideas, but, as Mallarmé reminded Degas, poems are not made out of ideas; they are made out of words. Joan Miró expressed the same concept from the painter's perspective: 'I try to apply colours like words that shape poems, like notes that shape music.' Susan Sontag may have had this in mind when she told her diary, 'I think I am ready to learn how to write. Think with words. Not with ideas.'

In the poem opening his *Collected Poems*, Yeats proclaimed, 'words alone are certain good'. Trying to explain to himself his endless quest for Maud Gonne, he wrote a poem entitled 'Words' that reveals how, for him, the great life force of Eros was inseparable from language. Reflecting on all the words he had used trying to persuade Gonne, he wondered what might have happened had he succeeded, and answered, 'I might have thrown poor words away / And been content to live'. Toward the end of his life, as he looked death in the eye, his impulse was to tame death with words by composing his epitaph and announcing it in a poem that describes his tombstone and declares, on its face, 'By his command these words are cut'. In life, love and death, words alone were certain good.

Focusing on some of Yeats's words enlarges the imagination and pulls us more deeply into life. This is what William Carlos Williams had in mind when he wrote in 'Asphodel, That Greeny Flower':

> It is difficult
> to get the news from poems
> yet men die miserably every day
> for lack
> of what is found there.

On Friendship

Think where man's glory most begins and ends,
And say my glory was I had such friends

At about the time Yeats wrote these lines in 'The Municipal Gallery Revisited', he told the audience at a banquet that, during a recent visit to the gallery, he had been 'overwhelmed with emotion' at the sight of 'pictures painted by men, now dead, who were once my intimate friends', and 'portraits of my fellow workers'.

The poem brings to life 'the images of thirty years', a pantheon of 'an Ireland / The poets have imagined, terrible and gay'. Here are John Synge, 'that rooted man'; Lady Augusta Gregory exuding 'all that pride and that humility'; Hugh Lane, the 'onlie begetter' of the gallery; Arthur Griffith 'staring in hysterical pride'; and Kevin O'Higgins, his 'soul incapable of remorse or rest'. Yeats's words caught the ear of Samuel Beckett. Late in life, he struggled to remember Yeats's capsule biography of Synge. Poet Anne Atik found 'that rooted man' in this poem.

It is no overstatement to apply to Yeats's verbal sketches Shakespeare's prediction in Sonnet 18:

> So long as men can breathe or eyes can see,
> So long lives this, and this gives life to thee.

The poem tempts us to have the fun of describing it with the Greek-based adjective for a poem about a painting, *ekphrastic*. But the poem is not so much about paintings as about the friends depicted in the paintings, or, more broadly, about friendship itself.

3

The closing couplet (quoted above) hovers above the particulars with a general statement that enables a speaker to honour friends by basking in their reflected glory.

The portrait of John Synge pictured here was painted by the poet's father, John Butler Yeats, who maintained that 'the best portraits will be painted where the relationship between the painter and the subject is one of friendship'. In fact, he went so far as to insist, 'I can only paint friendship portraits.'

'that rooted man': John Butler Yeats, *John Millington Synge*, reg. no. 54, collection and image © Hugh Lane Gallery, Dublin.

Friendship is all the house I have

Cicero's enduring essay *De Amicitia* tells us that friendship 'projects a bright ray of hope into the future, and upholds the spirit which otherwise might falter or grow faint'. Hearing that his friend Lady Gregory was seriously ill in February 1909, Yeats sought a much-needed ray of hope by writing a remarkable passage in his journal in which he exalted friendship above family and defined it as home.

When Yeats wrote about Gregory's illness he had never had a permanent home. As he was growing up, his father, a portrait painter, had financial difficulties, which Yeats attributed to an 'infirmity of will' that kept him from finishing a painting. The family moved from one rented premises to another, and from the time Yeats moved out on his own in the early 1890s until his marriage in 1917 at age fifty-two, he lived in rented rooms.

Against this background, Yeats wrote of Gregory's illness that 'more than kin was at stake'. Omitting reference to his father, he noted that Gregory 'has been to me mother, friend, sister and brother. I cannot realize the world without her – she brought to my wavering thoughts steadfast nobility. All day the thought of losing her is like a conflagration in the rafters. Friendship is all the house I have.'

Wandering Yeats turned Gregory's friendship into a house. His deft use of words is an extreme instance of the phenomenon observed by philosopher Gaston Bachelard in *The Poetics of Space*

'all that pride and that humility': Antonio Mancini, *Lady Gregory*, reg. no. 44, collection and image © Hugh Lane Gallery, Dublin.

that the idea of home is so powerful that 'wherever the human being has found the slightest shelter, we shall see the imagination build "walls" of impalpable shadows'.

The depth of Yeats's reaction to Gregory's illness engendered his poem 'A Friend's Illness':

Sickness brought me this
Thought, in that scale of his:
Why should I be dismayed
Though flame had burned the whole
World, as it were a coal,
Now I have seen it weighed
Against a soul?

Yeats sent this 'scrap of verse' to Gregory, explaining that what he meant by sickness and the scales was that, 'when one we love is ill we weigh them against a world without them'.

*no thought ... Could ever come between
Mind and delighted mind*

In these lines Yeats is describing his relationship with one of the three subjects of his poem 'Friends'. Its dramatic opening sets the stage for a meditation on three women and the joy, delight, ecstasy and sweetness they brought to his creative life:

Now must I these three praise –
Three women that have wrought
What joy is in my days:

This impulse to praise friends reflects a general Yeatsian tendency captured in critic Graham Hough's observation, 'No poet in our day has written more about his family and his friends than Yeats, and no one has been more successful in enlarging them to heroic proportions.' The three friends of the poem are Augusta Gregory, Olivia Shakespear and Maud Gonne. Shakespear was Yeats's first lover but he left her to resume his long quest for the unattainable Maud Gonne. The deep friendship between Yeats and Shakespear, although interrupted, continued until her death in 1938, just months before Yeats's own death. The delight generated by Shakespear lingers in this salute to friend and lover:

> One because no thought,
> Nor those unpassing cares,
> No, not in these fifteen
> Many-times-troubled years,
> Could ever come between
> Mind and delighted mind;

After Long Silence

In his unpublished memoirs Yeats tried to understand why he turned away from Olivia Shakespear. He couldn't resist, he wrote, 'the old lure', the Siren call of Maud Gonne. He explained it this way:

> All our lives long, as da Vinci says, we long, thinking it is but the moon that we long [for], for our destruction, and how, when we meet [it] in the shape of a most fair woman, can we do less than leave all others for her? Do we not seek dissolution upon her lips?

He told the story more simply and poignantly in a poem addressed to Gonne, but dominated by earlier memories. He called it 'The Lover mourns for the Loss of Love':

Pale brows, still hands and dim hair,
I had a beautiful friend
And dreamed that the old despair
Would end in love in the end:
She looked in my heart one day
And saw your image was there;
She has gone weeping away.

Reminiscing in 1926, nearly thirty years after Shakespear went 'weeping away', Yeats wrote to tell her, 'I came upon two early photographs of you yesterday, while going through my file – one from "Literary Year Book". Who ever had a like profile? – a profile from a Sicilean coin. One looks back to one's youth as to [a] cup that a mad man dying of thirst left half tasted. I wonder if you feel like that.'

The conversation continued in person. 'After Long Silence' tells the story:

Speech after long silence; it is right,
All other lovers being estranged or dead,
Unfriendly lamplight hid under its shade,
The curtains drawn upon unfriendly night,
That we descant and yet again descant
Upon the supreme theme of Art and Song:
Bodily decrepitude is wisdom; young
We loved each other and were ignorant.

The love and friendship embodied in this poem reflect a different Yeats from the poet envisioned by Nick, a character in Sally Rooney's novel *Conversations with Friends* who asserts that 'No one who likes Yeats is capable of human intimacy.'

friendship never ends

This line comes from Yeats's meditation on friendships that endured beyond the grave, 'All Souls' Night'. The poem, set in Oxford, jumps to life with this opening:

> Midnight has come, and the great Christ Church Bell
> And many a lesser bell sound through the room;
> And it is All Souls' Night,

Olivia Shakespear from *Literary Year Book*, 1897: 'young / We loved each other and were ignorant'.

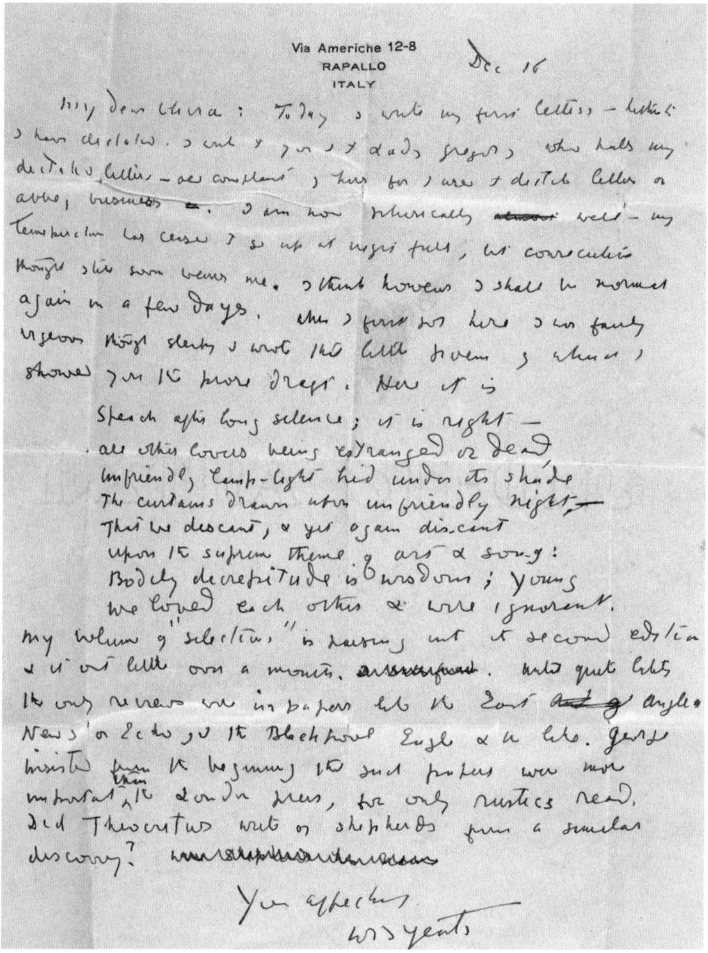

Via Americhe 12-8
RAPALLO
ITALY

Dec 16

My dear Olivia: To day I write my first letters — letters I have dictated. I cant [illegible] George who holds my dictated letters — all complaint I have for I were to dictate letters on other business. I am now physically [illegible] well — my temperature has ceased to go up at night fall, but consecutive thought still soon wearies me. I think however I shall be normal again in a few days. When I first got here I was fairly vigorous though sleepy I wrote this little poem of which I showed you the prose draft. Here it is

Speech after long silence; it is right —
All other lovers being estranged or dead,
Unfriendly lamp-light hid under its shade
The curtains drawn upon unfriendly night, —
That we descant, & yet again descant
Upon the supreme theme of art & song:
Bodily decrepitude is wisdom; young
We loved each other & were ignorant.

My volume of "selections" is passing into its second edition & it is out little over a month. [illegible]. [illegible] the only reviews were in papers like the East Anglian News or Echo, or the Blackpool Eagle & the like. George insisted from the beginning that such papers were more important than the London press, for only rustics read. Did Theocritus write of shepherds from a similar discovery? [illegible]

Yours affectionately
WB Yeats

Letter in which Yeats sends 'After Long Silence' to Olivia Shakespear.
Courtesy of the National Library of Ireland.

Among those summoned is MacGregor Mathers, of whom Yeats says:

> I thought him half a lunatic, half knave,
> And told him so, but friendship never ends;

The poet is able to summon the spirits of dead friends because the veil between the living and the dead is particularly thin on All Souls' Night, the last of three related commemorations of the dead in the calendar of the Christian Church. It is preceded by the celebration of All Saints' Day (also known as All Hallows) and its vigil, All Hallows' Eve, or Halloween.

In Ireland, these Christian customs were superimposed on the ancient Celtic feast of Samhain, celebrated from 31 October to 1 November, a liminal time when the boundary between this world and the other world is porous. Yeats explained the continuing force of Celtic belief in 'A General Introduction for My Work': 'Behind all Irish history hangs a great tapestry, even Christianity had to accept it and be itself pictured there. Nobody looking at its dim folds can say where Christianity begins and Druidism ends'.

Despite a rupture in their joint pursuit of occult ritual, Mathers retained the status of 'friend' because friendship never ends, even at death.

Printed text of Yeats's 11 October 1936 BBC broadcast 'Modern Poetry' inscribed to 'Olivia from her oldest friend WBY'.

Two girls in silk kimonos, both
Beautiful, one a gazelle

Friendship never ended for the two women recalled with both affection and bitterness in 'In Memory of Eva Gore-Booth and Con Markiewicz'. They are fixed forever in 'The light of evening, Lissadell, / Great windows open to the south'.

The poem contains the truths that 'a raving autumn shears / Blossom from the summer's wreath' and 'The innocent and the beautiful / Have no enemy but time'. Beginning languorously and ending in an explosion, it is quintessentially a poem to be read aloud.

Constance Gore-Booth in London, *circa* 1893, with Althea Gyles.
Photo courtesy of Sir Josslyn Gore-Booth and the Deputy Keeper
of the Records, the Public Record Office of Northern Ireland
(PRONI catalogue reference number D4131/K/4/1/19).

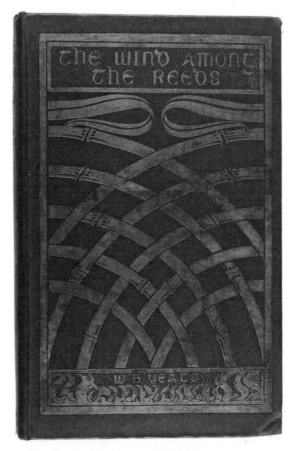

Cover design by Althea Gyles.

Leonard Cohen memorably opened his performance at Lissadell in 2010 by reciting the first four lines of this poem, then commenting that when he first read them more than fifty years previously in his home town of Montreal, 'I never knew that my steps would lead me to this place' and to 'being sheltered in the spirit of the great master whose lines I just quoted'.

The poem's explosive finale is just as memorable as its opening:

We the great gazebo built,
They convicted us of guilt;
Bid me strike a match and blow.

Implicitly reminding us that poems are made of words, Paul Muldoon's '7, Middagh Street' describes 'two girls in silk kimonos ... / Both beautiful, one a gazebo'.

Friends that have been friends indeed

The importance of friendship to Yeats is apparent from the prominent place he assigned to it when summing up his life's achievements in the late poem 'What Then?' The gift of 'Friends that have been friends indeed' is mentioned even before 'A small old house, wife, daughter, son' and just after 'Sufficient money for his need' and 'Everything he wrote was read'.

The proximity of 'friends indeed' to the poet's expression of pride in his readership suggests that the relationship between reader and writer is one of friendship. Yeats had made this idea explicit as early as his first volume of autobiography, *Reveries Over Childhood and Youth*, in 1915.

In his short preface to *Reveries*, Yeats notes that, in talking over incidents of the past, he sometimes noticed that his listener was bored, but rejoices that, 'now that I have written it all out, because one can always close a book, my friend need not be bored'. Solidifying the notion of friendship between author and reader, Yeats dedicated the volume to 'those few people mainly personal friends who have read all that I have written'.

Hearers and hearteners of the work

In 'At Galway Races', Yeats stresses the importance of friends as 'hearers and hearteners' of the poet's work – an idea applicable generally to the energy unleashed by the solidarity of friends:

> There where the course is,
> Delight makes all of the one mind,
> The riders upon the galloping horses,
> The crowd that closes in behind:
> We, too, had good attendance once,
> Hearers and hearteners of the work …

STEPPING STONES

INTERVIEWS WITH

SEAMUS HEANEY

Seamus Heaney

for Joe –
' hearer and heartener '

July 2009

THE MOMENT ALIVE

Eternal beauty wandering on her way

This line from 'To the Rose upon the Rood of Time' shows the young poet striving to find permanence in the rush of time by infusing the secular with the sacred. The arresting title implies that the rose of eternal beauty has been made flesh and crucified on the cross of time. The speaker beseeches the red rose:

> Come near, that no more blinded by man's fate,
> I find under the boughs of love and hate,
> In all poor foolish things that live a day,
> Eternal beauty wandering on her way.

The poem does what film-maker Jean Renoir praised in his father's paintings: 'find[ing] the relationship between eternity and the instant, between the world and the soul'.

Yeats emphasized the significance of the rose by making it a visual part of his readers' experience. Sturge Moore's design for the cover of *Per Amica Silentia Lunae* portrays the eternal beauty of the rose and the thorns that link it to the earth. The thorns evoke Christ's crown of thorns and thus the rood of time. The book's puzzling title highlights Yeats's obliquely phrased suggestion in the book that he sought inspiration from the Wisdom goddess symbolized by the moon. Borrowing a phrase from Virgil's account of the Greeks approaching Troy by the friendly quiet of the silent moon, he wrote that he had 'put myself to school where all things are seen: *A Tenedo tacitae per amica silentia lunae*'.

Cover design by Sturge Moore. Courtesy Special Collections,
James Joyce Library, University College Dublin.

The cover of Yeats's 1897 volume *The Secret Rose* even more
graphically focused the reader's eye on the conjunction of rose
and cross. It was designed by Althea Gyles to look like a textbook
of magic called a grimoire.

Yeats wrote of Gyles in the December 1898 issue of *The Dome* that 'her inspiration is a wave of a hidden tide that is flowing through many minds in many places, creating a new religious art and poetry'. The ethereal quality of Gyles as a person is captured in Yeats's comment to Florence Farr that she 'collects the necessities of life from her friends and spends her own money on flowers'.

Cover design by Althea Gyles. Courtesy Special Collections, James Joyce Library, University College Dublin.

For one throb of the artery

'A Meditation in Time of War' suggests that eternal beauty can be accessed instantaneously because transcendent experience can occur in 'one throb of the artery':

> For one throb of the artery,
> While on that old grey stone I sat
> Under the old wind-broken tree,
> I knew that One is animate
> Mankind inanimate phantasy.

These lines adapt Blake's pronouncement that 'the Poet's Work is Done; and all the Great / Events of Time start forth & are conceiv'd ... / Within a moment, a Pulsation of the Artery'. Yeats returns again and again to the idea that the moment is, as Ian Fletcher put it, 'the unit of experience, isolated, absolute, flexible in protest against the "positive" fiction of a stable world'.

Virginia Woolf's character Mrs Dalloway effortlessly captures the moment: 'the strange high singing of some aeroplane overhead was what she loved; life; London; this moment of June'.

Seamus Heaney was fond of one of the great celebrations of momentariness, Robert Graves's 'Sick Love':

> O Love, be fed with apples while you may,
> And feel the sun and go in royal array, ...

Take your delight in momentariness,
Walk between dark and dark – a shining space
With the grave's narrowness, though not its peace.

Heaney recited Graves's poem at the celebration of the 450th anniversary of Oxford's St John's College. Later, referring to his recovery from an illness, he wrote in a November 2006 letter, '"I feel the sun and go in rich array" – in *healthy* love.'

And twenty minutes more or less
It seemed, so great my happiness,
That I was blessed and could bless.

This fourth section of 'Vacillation' responds to a question posed at the poem's outset: 'What is joy?' The answer is not a philosophical disquisition, but a description of a moment of transcendence:

My fiftieth year had come and gone,
I sat, a solitary man,
In a crowded London shop,
An open book and empty cup
On the marble table-top.

While on the shop and street I gazed
My body of a sudden blazed;
And twenty minutes more or less
It seemed, so great my happiness,
That I was blessed and could bless.

The poem illustrates Walter Pater's dictum that 'success in life' is to achieve 'some mood of passion or insight or intellectual excitement' that is 'irresistibly real and attractive' and to 'burn always with this hard, gem-like flame'. No wonder critic Stefan Collini classifies poets with 'mathematicians, logicians [and] sprinters' as 'specialists in intensity'.

Yeats's description of his experience invites the reader to seek the same transcendence in the everyday, the same sacralizing of secular experience.

He noted in his diary a provocative comment by his friend, collaborator and lover, Florence Farr, about moments of intense happiness:

> Florence Farr once said to me, 'If we could say to ourselves, with sincerity, "This passing moment is as good as any I shall ever know", we would die upon the instant, or be united to God'. Desire would have ceased, and logic the feet of desire.

Everything that man esteems
Endures a moment or a day

This song from Yeats's play *The Resurrection* emphasizes the transience of the moment. It continues with illustrations of this recurring thought:

> Love's pleasure drives his love away,
> The painter's brush consumes his dreams;
> The herald's cry, the soldier's tread

> Exhaust his glory and his might:
> Whatever flames upon the night
> Man's own resinous heart has fed.

Man is in love and loves what vanishes,
What more is there to say?

Written in the wake of war's destruction, these lines from 'Nine-teen Hundred and Nineteen' address the poem's implicit question whether there is room for poetry in a world capable of horrific evil. Like Beckett's character in *The Unnamable* who proclaims, 'I can't go on, I'll go on,' Yeats goes on, buoyed by his belief in the power of words.

Words alone are certain good

Fleeting moments of transcendence would be lost if not captured in words.

'The Song of the Happy Shepherd', the earliest poem that Yeats included in his *Collected Poems*, proclaims the unique importance of words:

> Of all the many changing things
> In dreary dancing past us whirled,
> To the cracked tune that Chronos sings,
> Words alone are certain good.

Words persist in the face of time, which no longer flows harmoniously, but is 'the cracked tune that Chronos sings'. We needn't speculate that Yeats foresaw the insight of twentieth century physics that gravity causes time to lose its universality and unity. It was enough that the 'grey truth' of Darwinism undercut the majesty of time. As Yeats put it in the opening lines of 'Words':

> The woods of Arcady are dead,
> And over is their antique joy;
> Of old the world on dreaming fed;
> Grey Truth is now her painted toy;

In the context of time as a cracked tune, the written word can give permanence to experience: words alone are certain good. Yeats's acquaintance Vita Sackville-West put the idea memorably: 'It is necessary to write, if the days are not to slip emptily by. How else, indeed, to clap the net over the butterfly of the moment?'

A stanza in the original version of W.H. Auden's 'In Memory of W.B. Yeats' paid tribute to Yeats's belief in the enduring power of words by declaring that words can vanquish time:

> Time that is intolerant
> Of the brave and the innocent,
> And indifferent in a week
> To a beautiful physique,
>
> Worships language and forgives
> Everyone by whom it lives;
> Pardons cowardice, conceit,
> Lays its honours at their feet.

I will arise and go now, and go to Innisfree

Yeats shows how to put the moment into words in 'The Lake Isle of Innisfree'. The sound of bubbling water on a busy London street reminded him of the island of Innisfree, near his childhood home in Sligo, and kindled his desire to live there in imitation of Henry David Thoreau, who famously 'went to the woods because [he] wished to live deliberately'.

Yeats threw the net over this butterfly of a moment with these words:

> I will arise and go now, and go to Innisfree,
> And a small cabin build there, of clay and wattles made:
> Nine bean-rows will I have there, a hive for the honey-bee,
> And live alone in the bee-loud glade.
>
> And I shall have some peace there, for peace comes dropping
>   slow,
> Dropping from the veils of the morning to where the cricket
>   sings;
> There midnight's all a glimmer, and noon a purple glow,
> And evening full of the linnet's wings.
>
> I will arise and go now, for always night and day
> I hear lake water lapping with low sounds by the shore;
> While I stand on the roadway, or on the pavements grey,
> I hear it in the deep heart's core.

Yeats's words lock this moment in the memory. As poet Jane Hirshfield says, 'The Lake Isle of Innisfree' is a 'work that sounds like water over rocks or wind in trees', and by the time we hear the line 'I hear lake water lapping with low sounds by the shore', it is 'the lake itself to which we listen'.

When Wallace Stevens was looking for words that were clearly identifiable speech as opposed to meaningless natural sounds, he borrowed from 'The Lake Isle of Innisfree'. In 'Page from a Tale', the character Hans, hearing 'loud water and loud wind', registers the difference

> … between sound without meaning and speech,
> *Of clay and wattles made* as it ascends
> And *hear it* as it falls *in the deep heart's core.*

Innisfree is the tiny island below and to the right of the words 'Church Is.d' on this 1837 Ordnance Survey of Ireland map.

WORKING

The intellect of man is forced to choose
Perfection of the life, or of the work

The poet Rainer Maria Rilke had also wrestled with the dilemma Yeats describes in these lines from 'The Choice'. After a long conversation in 1902 with Auguste Rodin, in which the sculptor insisted that 'it is necessary to work, nothing but work', Rilke wrote to his wife, 'one must choose either this or that. Either happiness or art ... The great men have all let their lives become overgrown like an old road and have carried everything into their art. Their lives are stunted like an organ they no longer need.'

Six years later, after having worked as Rodin's secretary, Rilke decided to focus on writing, and published the mesmeric sonnet 'Archaic Torso of Apollo'. The first thirteen lines describe in electrifying detail the headless torso 'still suffused with brilliance from inside, / like a lamp' since 'Otherwise / the curved chest could not dazzle you so'. Rilke then transforms the fragment into the basis for a complete poem by ending abruptly with the injunction, 'You must change your life.' The commanding voice could belong to Apollo (the god of art), Rodin, Rilke himself, or an amalgam of all three.

Yeats's 'The Choice', one of his most ringing pronouncements, originated in 1932 as a stanza in a long poem about his friendship with Lady Gregory, 'Coole Park and Ballylee', but was excised to stand on its own.

The stately cadence of iambic pentameter gives Yeats's lines an oracular force. Even so, the reader is free to resist. In fact, the lines seem to invite resistance. Novelist and essayist Zadie Smith responded to the poem by questioning, 'Why must either life or work be perfect?' Rather, she argued, we are all 'stumbling through this world, constantly re-examining the checks and balances of [our] choices, knowing that they are helping here but hurting there'.

Still, Smith recognizes the usefulness of Yeats's formulation of the tension between work and life. 'I feel extremely fortunate', she writes, 'to be engaged in this lifelong project concerning their inter-relation, communication, mutual rejection and argument.'

In the course of totting up his accomplishments in the 1936 poem 'What Then?', Yeats made clear that he had chosen perfection of the work, proclaiming, 'I swerved in nought, / Something to perfection brought'.

this accustomed toil

In 'All Things can Tempt me', the poet pessimistically sees his life as no more than 'this accustomed toil' of the 'craft of verse':

> All things can tempt me from this craft of verse:
> One time it was a woman's face, or worse –
> The seeming needs of my fool-driven land;
> Now nothing but comes readier to the hand
> Than this accustomed toil. When I was young,
> I had not given a penny for a song
> Did not the poet sing it with such airs
> That one believed he had a sword upstairs;
> Yet would be now, could I but have my wish,
> Colder and dumber and deafer than a fish.

The last line echoes in Paul Muldoon's moving elegy *Incantata*, whose subject, the artist Mary Farl Powers, lies 'colder and dumber than a fish by Francisco de Herrera'.

The Fascination of What's Difficult

In the poem with this title, work's difficulty can be fascinating, but the rest of life is consigned to a state resembling the 'atrophied organ' described by Rilke:

> The fascination of what's difficult
> Has dried the sap out of my veins, and rent
> Spontaneous joy and natural content
> Out of my heart.

Still, difficult work *is* fascinating. The response of the Roman philosopher Seneca to a friend's complaint about the shortness of life is a reminder of the value of fascinating work. In his essay 'On the Shortness of Life' Seneca wrote that 'learning how to live takes a whole life' and 'it is not that we have a short time to live, but that we waste a lot of it'. Zadie Smith agrees: 'I think Seneca is right: life feels longer the more you engage with it.'

we must labour to be beautiful

In 'Adam's Curse' Yeats recognizes the hard work needed to create beauty. He is told,

> 'To be born woman is to know –
> Although they do not talk of it at school –
> That we must labour to be beautiful.'

He responds:

> I said: 'It's certain there is no fine thing
> Since Adam's fall but needs much labouring.'

Yeats's meditation on the relationship between labour and beauty led him to embrace what he called 'Castiglione's saying that the physical beauty of woman is the spoil or monument of the victory of the soul … the result of emotional toil in past lives'.

Seamus Heaney admired Yeats's 'tough-minded insight that all reality comes to us as the reward of labour'.

Yeats found a way to harmonize the competing claims of labour and joy, at least for those fortunate to find work they enjoy or to learn to enjoy the work that finds them.

Labouring in ecstasy

'Friends' praises Lady Augusta Gregory because she

> So changed me that I live
> Labouring in ecstasy.

This paean to the transformative power of Gregory's steadfast example bears out Cicero's observation, 'He who looks upon a true friend, looks, as it were, upon a better image of himself.'

Yeats elaborated on the meaning of the paradoxical notion of 'labouring in ecstasy' in 'Among School Children', where he declared:

> Labour is blossoming or dancing where
> The body is not bruised to pleasure soul,
> Nor beauty born out of its own despair,
> Nor blear-eyed wisdom out of midnight oil,

Yeats's decision to locate this insight 'among schoolchildren' calls to mind Ben Lerner's observation that children are poets in the sense that they don't 'observe a clear distinction between what counts as labor and what counts as leisure'.

The many suggestions we hear for achieving work-life balance reflect the assumption that work and joy are fundamentally inconsistent, an idea as old as the biblical story that Adam was forced to earn his bread by the sweat of his brow as punishment for primal disobedience. Yeats's talismanic phrase 'labouring in ecstasy' heals this split.

Making Your Soul

Now shall I make my soul

'Vacillation' grapples with the conundrum pinpointed by Henry David Thoreau when, using the eye-catching phrase 'up garret', he wrote in *Walden*, 'This spending of the best part of one's life earning money in order to enjoy a questionable liberty during the least valuable part of it reminds me of the Englishman who went to India to make a fortune first, in order that he might return to England and live the life of a poet. He should have gone up garret at once.'

After completing studies in modern languages and medieval history at Oxford in 1915, Dorothy L. Sayers took something of a Thoreau-like approach to building an independent life as a writer. She eschewed the traditional role of teacher on the ground that it was 'immoral to take up a job solely for the amount of time one can spend away from it'.

Yeats addressed the Thoreau conundrum with the idea of living, as he said in a letter to Olivia Shakespear, 'like one of those Japanese who in the middle ages retired from the world at 50 or so ... to devote himself "to art and letters" which was considered sacred'. Yeats announces such a decision in 'The Tower', declaring,

> Now shall I make my soul,
> Compelling it to study
> In a learned school
> Till the wreck of body,
> Slow decay of blood,

Testy delirium
Or dull decrepitude,
Or what worse evil come –

Yeats's words profoundly engaged Samuel Beckett. Returning from the cremation of his old friend Con Leventhal in Paris in 1979, Beckett stopped, leaned against a wall, and, a glass of wine in his hand, recited the above lines, then hesitated, squared his shoulders and finished the quotation:

The death of friends, or death
Of every brilliant eye
That made a catch in the breath –
Seem but the clouds of the sky …

Followers of pyschologist Erik Erikson have located the seventh stage of psychological development, in which generativity struggles against stagnation, between the ages of forty and sixty-five. Dante was in his early forties when he set out on the great inward journey recounted in *The Divine Comedy*. At the outset of what is perhaps the greatest work of Western literature, he stressed that it was in the middle of the journey of our life (*nel mezzo del cammin di nostra vita*) that he found himself in a dark wood, and began his journey through the mysteries of the afterlife.

Montaigne chose age thirty-eight as the time to escape from what he called 'the servitude of the court and of public employment', and retire, as he inscribed in Latin on the wall of his tower, 'to the bosom of the learned virgins [Muses], where in calm and freedom from all cares' he will complete his life.

In 'Vacillation' Yeats opted for age forty as the time to make your soul. He measured the forty years from the time that, as the Neo-Platonists posited, the soul in the process of incarnation cleansed the memory of past lives by drinking from the river Lethe's water of forgetfulness. Forty years after being caught 'in Lethean foliage', it is time for the soul to prepare to exit the body once again:

> No longer in Lethean foliage caught
> Begin the preparation for your death
> And from the fortieth winter by that thought
> Test every work of intellect or faith,
> And everything that your own hands have wrought,
> And call those works extravagance of breath
> That are not suited for such men as come
> Proud, open-eyed and laughing to the tomb.

A king is but a foolish labourer
Who wastes his blood to be another's dream

King Fergus speaks these words to the druid in the poem 'Fergus and the Druid'. It is no surprise, then, when Fergus gives this answer to the druid's query as to what he wants:

> Be no more a king,
> But learn the dreaming wisdom that is yours.

Fergus's answer gives the imprimatur of Celtic mythology to Yeats's idea of retiring from the world to make his soul.

animate
The trivial days and ram them with the sun

What of the time before your fortieth winter? Thoreau seemed to think one couldn't work for a living without forfeiting an inner life. In 'Vacillation' Yeats declares otherwise: 'Get all the gold and silver that you can,' he counsels, but 'animate / The trivial days and ram them with the sun.'

The use of the word ram echoes Ben Jonson's comment about Shakespeare, which Yeats had slightly modified in an essay in which he said, 'Surely of the passionate dead we can but cry in words Ben Jonson meant for none but Shakespeare: "So rammed" are they "with life they can but grow in life with being."'

Yeats appends several memorable maxims to the basic advice:

> Get all the gold and silver that you can,
> Satisfy ambition, animate
> The trivial days and ram them with the sun,
> And yet upon these maxims meditate:
> All women dote upon an idle man
> Although their children need a rich estate;
> No man has ever lived that had enough
> Of children's gratitude or woman's love.

LOVING

And no more turn aside and brood
Upon love's bitter mystery

Yeats believed that 'if a man is to write lyric poetry he must be shaped by nature and art to some one out of half a dozen traditional roles, and be lover or saint, sage or sensualist, or mere mocker of all life'. Early on, he made a fundamental choice that many of his poems would be written in the role of lover. Enthusiastically adopting that role, he introduced 'love's bitter mystery' into another poem about the legendary Fergus, who gave up his kingship to pursue the knowledge of the Druids. These lines follow those quoted above in 'Who Goes with Fergus?':

> For Fergus rules the brazen cars,
> And rules the shadows of the wood,
> And the white breast of the dim sea
> And all dishevelled wandering stars.

James Joyce, then a student at University College Dublin, heard this lyric in Yeats's play *The Countess Cathleen* on the opening night of what became the Abbey Theatre. He thought it the most beautiful lyric he'd ever heard and set it to music. It spoke to him at such a deep level that he sang it to his dying fourteen-year-old brother Georgie, and placed it at the emotional centre of *Ulysses*. In the novel, Joyce's alter-ego Stephen has refused his mother's plea that he pray at her death-bed, but has this memory when he hears Buck Mulligan singing, 'No more turn aside and brood':

Fergus' song: I sang it alone in the house, holding down the long dark chords. Her door was open: she wanted to hear my music. Silent with awe and pity I went to her bedside. She was crying in her wretched bed. For those words, Stephen: love's bitter mystery.

She bid me take love easy

In October 1904 James Joyce shared the stage at a concert with the great tenor John McCormack in the Ancient Concert Rooms. *The Freeman's Journal* praised his 'sweet tenor voice', which he wrapped around the words of Yeats's 'Down by the Salley Gardens'.

> Down by the salley gardens
>   my love and I did meet;
> She passed the salley gardens
>   with little snow-white feet.
> She bid me take love easy,
>   as the leaves grow on the tree;
> But I, being young and foolish,
>   with her would not agree.
>
> In a field by the river
>   my love and I did stand,
> And on my leaning shoulder
>   she laid her snow-white hand.
> She bid me take life easy,
>   as the grass grows on the weirs;
> But I was young and foolish,
>   and now am full of tears.

Nora Barnacle, who famously had her first sexual experience with Joyce the previous June on the day now celebrated as 'Bloomsday', attended the concert. Soon after the October concert, she left Dublin with Joyce for an uncertain future in continental Europe. Joyce and Nora were both young, arguably foolish, and neither took love easy.

Joyce and Nora eventually moved to Paris, where Joyce often recited Yeats's poems from memory to his friends.

Ah, penny, brown penny, brown penny,
One cannot begin it too soon

These are the concluding lines of a poem that was originally entitled 'The Young Man's Song' but was so dominated by its refrain that Yeats re-named it 'Brown Penny'. The new name seems to assert itself as the poem emerges:

> I whispered, 'I am too young.'
> And then, 'I am old enough';
> Wherefore I threw a penny
> To find out if I might love.
> 'Go and love, go and love, young man,
> If the lady be young and fair.'
> Ah, penny, brown penny, brown penny,
> I am looped in the loops of her hair.
>
> O love is the crooked thing,
> There is nobody wise enough
> To find out all that is in it,

For he would be thinking of love
Till the stars had run away
And the shadows eaten the moon.
Ah, penny, brown penny, brown penny,
One cannot begin it too soon.

Joyce and Nora were definitely of the 'One cannot begin it too soon' school.

Yeats, on the other hand, was finding his pleasure in the indecision and anticipation that led the young man of the poem to toss a coin to determine whether he was too young to become a lover.

Yeats waited until he was nearly thirty-one before experiencing sexual love and, indeed, as told in his private memoir, 'was startled and a little shocked' when Olivia Shakespear started him on the path to physical intimacy by punctuating their first railway journey by giving him 'the long passionate kiss of love'.

Until then, the apprentice who would become one of the great love poets of all time was content with what Tony Tanner, writing about Proust, called 'the indefinable and unconfinable pleasure of absence, a pleasure indistinguishable from pleasure deferred or that pleasure which is deferral'.

O Do Not Love Too Long

The poem with this title suggests a possible outcome that may have deterred the young man of 'Brown Penny' from starting down the path of love:

But O, in a minute she changed —
O do not love too long,
Or you will grow out of fashion
Like an old song.

Both this poem and 'Brown Penny' are songs of young men trying out and trying on possible attitudes toward love.

Does the imagination dwell the most Upon a woman won or woman lost?

Quantitative analysis provides an easy answer in Yeats's case to the piercing question he asks in 'The Tower'. He wrote many more poems about the woman lost, Maud Gonne, than about his first lover, Olivia Shakespear, or his wife, Georgie Hyde-Lees. Readers will have to do their own math to arrive at a personal answer.

That 'woman lost' would be the answer was a foregone conclusion for a poet writing in the courtly love tradition because the subject of such a poem was defined as 'the-woman-from-whom-one-is parted', and the inescapable Catch 22 was that 'to win her is to lose her'.

This explains Yeats's otherwise puzzling characterization of the occasion when he first met Gonne as the moment when 'the troubling of my life began'. The experience, he tantalizingly wrote, reverberated with 'a sound as of a Burmese gong, an over-powering tumult that had yet many pleasant secondary notes'.

Yeats's retrospective account of his initial meeting with Gonne reflects his desire to cast her in the image of Beatrice to his Dante.

The Tuscan poet had recounted in *La Vita Nuova* that merely being in the presence of Beatrice, but before seeing her, 'I seemed to feel a strange throbbing that began in the left side of my breast.' Yeats goes one better. He experiences 'premonitory excitement' upon first reading Gonne's name.

A hunger for the apple on the bough
Most out of reach

This image shows what Yeats could do with a fragment of a poem by the seventh-century BC Greek poet Sappho. He used it to characterize Dante's pursuit of Beatrice, but it fits his fascination for the unattainable Maud Gonne so perfectly that its appeal to Yeats must have been irresistible. Anne Carson's translation of Sappho both shows the power of Sappho's lines and permits us to see how Yeats upped the wattage by introducing the lover's hunger. Here is Carson's translation:

> as the sweetapple reddens on a high branch
> > high on the highest branch and the applepickers forgot –
> no, not forgot, were unable to reach

In 'Ego Dominus Tuus', Yeats placed Dante's hunger for unreachable Beatrice at the core of his identity. When the first voice in the poem lauds Dante for having 'so utterly found himself', the second voice asks this question about the distinctive image of Dante's hollow face:

And did he find himself
Or was the hunger that had made it hollow
A hunger for the apple on the bough
Most out of reach?

Maud Gonne, the apple on the bough most out of reach.

Essayist Brian Dillon's comment on fragments has interesting application to Yeats's transformation of Sappho. A fragment, says Dillon, arrives 'haloed by conjecture and mystery [and] stands alone but speaks, or must be made to speak by a reader, to the fragments that surround it'.

The gaps in the Sappho fragments bequeathed to us heighten their intense mystery. Perhaps it was the very incompleteness of Sappho's lines that attracted Yeats to them as a metaphor for his longing for Gonne. Historian Thomas Habinek suggests that the fragmentary character of what we have of Sappho's poetry 'serves as a reminder of the inevitable incompleteness of human knowledge and affection'.

Sappho may have been the inspiration for Auden's 'Eros, builder of cities' with her more intimate 'Eros the melter of limbs'. Memorably, Sappho coined the word bittersweet as applied to Eros. Carson says no one who has been in love disputes her.

Classicist Daniel Mendelsohn aptly characterizes Sappho's lyrics as having 'the emotional intensity, self-reflection and subjective expressiveness which we see as fundamental to lyric poetry'. One of Sappho's poems, apparently a song for a wedding, contains a line made famous as the title of J.D. Salinger's *Raise High the Roof Beam, Carpenters.*

When you are old and grey and full of sleep
And nodding by the fire

Experiencing the present by looking back at it from an imagined future, Yeats asks the vibrant Gonne to accept his poem today, and then, when old and grey, take down the book and remember that, among the many who loved her beauty with love false or true,

> ... one man loved the pilgrim soul in you,
> And loved the sorrows of your changing face;
>
> And bending down beside the glowing bars,
> Murmur, a little sadly, how Love fled
> And paced upon the mountains overhead
> And hid his face amid a crowd of stars.

This moving poem, 'When You are Old', experiments with the idea later articulated in Proust's observation that 'the true paradises are the paradises we have lost'. Seeking, as would Proust, the moment when past and present are identical, and thus outside time, Yeats manoeuvres his love for Gonne from past to future and back to the present.

Thus do poets give shape and clarity to such mysteries as the suggestion of theoretical physicist Carlo Rovelli that the distinction between past and future disappears at the microscopic state of things, and that our sense of being between past and future events – the 'flow' of time – is part of our mental structure. The world of physics is not so far removed from Yeats's poem, in which Love 'hid his face amid a crowd of stars'.

Yeats and Gonne were old hands at playing with the laws of physics. When she was in France and he in Ireland or England, they wrote to each other of their meetings 'on the astral plane', a realm midway between the material and spiritual worlds, where the history of their past could merge with the mystery of their future.

The astral plane, first defined by Paracelsus (1493–1541), a Swiss physician, alchemist and astrologer, was much visited by Yeats and other members of the theosophist Order of the Golden Dawn.

all that lamentation of the leaves

In 'The Sorrow of Love', without mentioning Maud Gonne or Helen of Troy by name, Yeats deals with his doomed pursuit of Gonne by seeing her as a mythical Helen and deflecting his own grief into a cosmic 'lamentation of the leaves'.

> The brawling of a sparrow in the eaves,
> The brilliant moon and all the milky sky,
> And all that famous harmony of leaves,
> Had blotted out man's image and his cry.
>
> A girl arose that had red mournful lips
> And seemed the greatness of the world in tears,
> Doomed like Odysseus and the labouring ships
> And proud as Priam murdered with his peers;

Arose, and on the instant clamorous eaves,
A climbing moon upon an empty sky,
And all that lamentation of the leaves,
Could but compose man's image and his cry.

A pity beyond all telling
Is hid in the heart of love

The rest of 'The Pity of Love' explains:

> The folk who are buying and selling,
> The clouds on their journey above,
> The cold wet winds ever blowing,
> And the shadowy hazel grove
> Where mouse-grey waters are flowing
> Threaten the head that I love.

The poem dashes what philosopher Martha Nussbaum calls 'the splendid and equivocal hope' of Greek thought that rationality could save the lover from the risk inherent in the beloved's vulnerability to luck. Yeats doesn't sugar-coat the risk but accepts, as did Aristotle, that a life so vulnerable is nonetheless the best.

And pluck till time and times are done
The silver apples of the moon,
The golden apples of the sun

In 'The Song of Wandering Aengus', the eponymous wanderer, the god of love,

> … went out to the hazel wood
> Because a fire was in my head,

He sees a glimmering girl with apple blossom in her hair, but she 'faded through the brightening air'. Yeats never forgot that when he first met Maud Gonne she was standing before a vase filled with apple blossom at a window. Gonne was thus on solid ground in claiming that the apple blossom was a clue that she was the glimmering girl. Aengus pledges unwavering pursuit:

> Though I am old with wandering
> Through hollow lands and hilly lands,
> I will find out where she has gone,
> And kiss her lips and take her hands;
> And walk among long dappled grass,
> And pluck till time and times are done
> The silver apples of the moon,
> The golden apples of the sun.

The concluding lines work their magic on Francesca in Robert James Waller's *The Bridges of Madison County*. A stranger introduces himself by reciting them and praising their 'realism, economy, sensuousness, beauty, magic'. Next thing you know, Francesca is tacking a note on the bridge inviting him to dinner. 'Got your note,' he replies, 'W.B. Yeats as a messenger and all that.'

I have spread my dreams under your feet;
Tread softly because you tread on my dreams

From 'He wishes for the Cloths of Heaven', this line is one of Yeats's signature sound bites. It comes from the short poem that, as mentioned in the introduction, enchanted Patti Smith at age five and made her a lifelong devotee of Yeats:

> Had I the heavens' embroidered cloths,
> Enwrought with golden and silver light,
> The blue and the dim and the dark cloths
> Of night and light and the half-light,
> I would spread the cloths under your feet:
> But I, being poor, have only my dreams;
> I have spread my dreams under your feet;
> Tread softly because you tread on my dreams.

The eight-line poem uses its simple words in ways that suggest they have power independent of their meaning. The words 'cloths', 'dreams' and 'light' appear three times and 'tread' and 'under your feet' twice.

Technically, there are no end-rhymes, but 'cloths', 'light', 'feet' and 'dreams' are each used twice at the end of a line. Internal rhymes like 'night', 'light', and 'half-light' in the fourth line further focus our attention on the sound of the words independent of their meaning. The combination of repetition and rhyme enchant with a spell in the manner that Yeats envisioned as the origin of poetry.

The poem reflects Yeats's great attention to the way his poems would be performed. It is written to be read in a very specific way. While the first half of the poem sings along rhythmically, the second is a series of statements and invocations that require the reader to pause dramatically at the end of each line. The words embody an immensely powerful dramatic trick, which surely contributes to the way the poem has echoed down the years.

When my arms wrap you round I press
My heart upon the loveliness
That has long faded from the world

This beautiful poem to Olivia Shakespear, 'He remembers Forgotten Beauty', caught the ear of James Joyce, whose character Stephen Dedalus asserts in *Portrait of the Artist as a Young Man* that he would rather 'press in my arms the loveliness which has not yet come into the world'.

George Russell, known as Æ, put his finger on the yin and yang of the Yeats-Joyce relationship when he wrote that Joyce was Yeats's spiritual and artistic son who was determined to 'balance in our national life an intense imagination of beauty, by an equally intense preoccupation with its dark and bitter opposite'.

> *that monstrous thing*
> *Returned and yet unrequited love*

Pursuit of the unattainable Gonne elicited great poetry, but left an imperfect life. The idea of courtly love is romantic in theory but in practice it can be, as Yeats says in these lines from 'Presences', monstrous. Yeats's *Memoirs* record Gonne's response to his proposal of marriage in 1891: 'No, she could not marry – there were reasons – she would never marry; but in words that had no conventional ring she asked for my friendship.' His love was thus in a sense returned, but unrequited.

> *So great a sweetness flows*
> *I shake from head to foot*

These rivetting lines praise Maud Gonne, the last of the three subjects of 'Friends'. Whereas the traditional Muse poem blames its subject for resisting the poet's pursuit, Yeats instead praises Gonne, revelling in the shattering intensity her memory brings at daybreak:

> And what of her that took
> All till my youth was gone
> With scarce a pitying look?
> How could I praise that one?

When day begins to break
I count my good and bad,
Being wakeful for her sake,
Remembering what she had,
What eagle look still shows,
While up from my heart's root
So great a sweetness flows
I shake from head to foot.

Beckett would read 'Friends' aloud and stand up as he repeated the last three lines in amazement, exclaiming, 'Imagine such feeling.'

Suddenly I meet your face

This powerful declaration of undiminished passion takes its title, 'A Deep-sworn Vow', from Yeats's belief that, although Gonne would not marry him, she had promised that neither would she marry anyone else. After Yeats was shocked by her marrying Major John MacBride, others, he says, 'have been friends of mine', but Gonne's ineradicable image invariably appears when he clambers to the heights of sleep or grows excited with wine:

Others because you did not keep
That deep-sworn vow have been friends of mine;
Yet always when I look death in the face,
When I clamber to the heights of sleep,
Or when I grow excited with wine,
Suddenly I meet your face.

Was there another Troy for her to burn?

Yeats continues on the path of suggesting that he has plenty of reason for blaming Gonne, but declining to do so. Again, he equates her with Helen of Troy, thus evoking both great beauty and the violence of the Trojan War. 'No Second Troy' opens with a question – 'Why should I blame her?' – and closes with a pair of answering questions:

> Why, what could she have done, being what she is?
> Was there another Troy for her to burn?

The question of blame also haunts 'Old Memory', where Yeats struggles with the urge to tell his thought to 'fly to her when the end of day / Awakens an old memory' of what he and Gonne might have accomplished together, but concludes, 'enough, / For when we have blamed the wind we can blame love'.

The Folly of Being Comforted

In a poem with this title, the poet's 'ever kind' friend (Augusta Gregory) points to signs that his unattainable beloved is ageing and so encourages him with the thought that 'Time can but make it easier to be wise.' 'No,' the poet cries,

> I have not a crumb of comfort, not a grain. ...

O heart! O heart! If she'd but turn her head,
You'd know the folly of being comforted.

The manuscript shows the courtly love poet carefully changing the 'crows feet' about his beloved's eyes to 'shadows'.

Manuscript of 'The Folly of Being Comforted'. Courtesy Special Collections, James Joyce Library, University College Dublin.

Never Give all the Heart

The poem with this title is an invitation to a dialogue, leaving us to accept or reject the speaker's premise:

Never give all the heart, for love
Will hardly seem worth thinking of
To passionate women if it seem
Certain, and they never dream
That it fades out from kiss to kiss;
For everything that's lovely is
But a brief, dreamy, kind delight.
O never give the heart outright,
For they, for all smooth lips can say,
Have given their hearts up to the play.
And who could play it well enough
If deaf and dumb and blind with love?
He that made this knows all the cost,
For he gave all his heart and lost.

The voice in the poem's opening line may be that of John Quinn, the New York lawyer and militantly confirmed bachelor with whom Yeats was staying when he wrote the poem in November 1903, and who later boasted of the 'iron determination' with which he maintained his unmarried state.

Yeats composed the poem in his head following a discussion with his host about, as Quinn later put it in a letter, 'whether a man should give himself unreservedly or act with a certain reservation' in matters of the heart. Yeats murmured the words to himself while they were *en route* to dinner, and wrote them out on a piece of paper when they reached the restaurant. He gave the paper to Quinn who retained this poem until his death, even though he sold most of his manuscripts. Yeats's gift of the manuscript may signal his understanding that it reflected Quinn's voice. Quinn's retention suggests that he heard his own voice in its words.

The poem can be viewed through the prism of Yeats's aphoristic description of his creative process: 'We make out of the quarrel with others, rhetoric, but of the quarrel with ourselves, poetry.' Perhaps 'Never Give All the Heart' begins in rhetoric and ends in poetry.

Many of Yeats's poems show him eschewing the opening line's prohibition, and instead giving all the heart.

I might have thrown poor words away
And been content to live

After years of fruitlessly wooing Maud Gonne with words designed to bring her around to his point of view, Yeats made this rueful observation in a poem entitled 'Words':

> That had she done so who can say
> What would have shaken from the sieve?
> I might have thrown poor words away
> And been content to live.

Hospitable Places

The trees are in their autumn beauty,
The woodland paths are dry

These opening lines of 'The Wild Swans at Coole' exhibit 'hospitality', the quality of a text that, as defined in a study of 'homes and haunts' of writers, 'seems to invite the reader to enter its originating milieu'. This poem invites us not only to enter Lady Gregory's beautiful Coole Park, but also to gain access to Yeats's interior life, as mirrored in the swans who 'drift on the still water / mysterious, beautiful' – emblems, as he wrote in 'Nineteen Hundred and Nineteen' and *A Vision*, of the solitary soul.

Cover design by Sturge Moore for the 1919
Macmillan edition of *The Wild Swans at Coole.*

Wild swans at Coole 'Upon the brimming water among the stones'.
Photo © Deirdre Holmes.

Written in October 1916 in the wake of Maud Gonne's rejection of his marriage proposal, the poem casts its author as the unmated nine and fiftieth swan. The hearts of the mated swans 'have not grown old':

> Passion or conquest, wander where they will,
> Attend upon them still.

But the poet's 'heart is sore', as the mated swans

> ... scatter wheeling in great broken rings
> Upon their clamorous wings.

Seeing his nineteenth autumn of temporary residence at Coole as paralleling the peripatetic swans, Yeats wonders:

> Among what rushes will they build,
> By what lake's edge or pool
> Delight men's eyes when I awake some day
> To find they have flown away?

The slate-grey lake near the Flaggy Shore. Photo © Deirdre Holmes.

Seamus Heaney's 'Postscript' finds the swans at the nearby Flaggy Shore. The poem echoes 'The Wild Swans at Coole' by describing autumnal beauty amidst water and stones, then sees that

> The surface of a slate-grey lake is lit
> By the earthed lightning of a flock of swans ...

The poem concludes by telling its author that he is 'A hurry through which known and strange things pass' while the wind catches the heart off guard and blows it open.

Heaney's remark that he might have called his poem 'The Wild Swans at Clare' is a testament to the power of Yeats's words both to capture the beauty of a place and to create a memorable symbol of the solitary soul.

Yeats's words hovered in Heaney's consciousness as his own poem came to him 'like a ball kicked in from nowhere: in this case', he told Dennis O'Driscoll, 'I was completely absorbed in writing one of the last of the Oxford lectures when I had this quick sidelong glimpse of something flying past; before I knew where I was, I went after it.'

And may these characters remain
When all is ruin once again

The poet of 'The Wild Swans at Coole' was a rejected suitor of no fixed abode in search of a wife and a home. The poem containing these lines, 'To be Carved on a Stone at Thoor Ballylee', announces that he has found both.

At age fifty-two, in 1917, Yeats married George Hyde-Lees and was restoring as a summer residence an ancient tower, Thoor Ballylee, that had been a part of Coole. The poem 'To be Carved on a Stone at Thoor Ballylee' ties the marriage and the tower together, and finds in them a sense of permanence:

> I, the poet William Yeats,
> With old mill boards and sea-green slates,
> And smithy work from the Gort forge,
> Restored this tower for my wife George;
> And may these characters remain
> When all is ruin once again.

Yeats's poem embodies his belief that his words are metaphorically carved in stone. Seamus Heaney linked the stones of Thoor Ballylee to Yeats's craft of verse when he praised Yeats's 'dream of phonetic masonry, squared and plumbed and dominant'.

Yeats's conviction of the stone-like longevity of his words differs from the sentiment reflected in the epitaph John Keats requested, 'Here lies one whose name was writ in water.'

Words etched in stone. Photo © Deirdre Holmes.

Robinson Jeffers, who visited Thoor Ballylee, and built a stone tower in California in imitation of Yeats, expressed a Yeats-like belief in the durability of his words in 'To the Stone-Cutters':

Stone-cutters fighting time with marble, you foredefeated
Challengers of oblivion
Eat cynical earnings, knowing rock splits, records fall down,
The square-limbed Roman letters
Scale in the thaws, wear in the rain. The poet as well

Builds his monument mockingly;
For man will be blotted out, the blithe earth die, the brave sun
Die blind and blacken to the heart:
Yet stones have stood for a thousand years, and pained
     thoughts found
The honey of peace in old poems.

In our world of evanescent electronic communication, Yeats's poem gives permanence to the idea that carefully crafted writing continues to exert influence long after its author's death. Jeffers' poem is a case in point.

The winding stairs at Thoor Ballylee. Photo © Deirdre Holmes.

Sturge Moore's cover design for *The Winding Stair.* Courtesy James Joyce Library, University College Dublin.

I declare this tower is my symbol

After these words in 'Blood and the Moon', Yeats further declares:

> This winding, gyring, spiring treadmill of a stair is my
> ancestral stair;
> That Goldsmith and the Dean, Berkeley and Burke have
> travelled there.

These twin pronouncements are illuminated by Yeats's comment in a letter to Sturge Moore, designer of the cover of the magnificent volumes *The Tower* and *The Winding Stair*. Yeats told Moore that his tower was a 'rooting of mythology in the earth'. By living in Thoor Ballylee, he was sinking his roots into Irish historical consciousness, where he found the great figures of eighteenth-century Anglo-Ireland.

Towers seem especially suited to calling up ancestors from a collective memory. Five years after Yeats moved into Thoor Ballylee, Carl Jung built a tower on the Upper Lake of Zurich at Bollingen. As Jung sank his roots into the depths, he sensed that the souls of his ancestors were gathering about his tower.

Moving into a tower is neither an option nor a goal for most of us, but Yeats's words are both a shorthand expression of the energy and strength that can be tapped by maintaining a psychological link with our ancestors, and a way of capturing the sense of purpose derived from identification with place. The place needn't be grand. For Virginia Woolf, a room of one's own sufficed; and, as Seamus Heaney's essays remind us, places of the mind can be more powerful than material surroundings.

The architecture of Yeats's poem, its formal structure, fixes its content in the reader's mind. Seamus Heaney admired this quality, writing, 'I like to remember, for example, that the word stanza comes from the Italian word for a room, and to find in the architectural sureness of stone rooms and winding stairs an image of the physicality and undislodgeableness of Yeats's poetic forms.'

The power of Yeats's forms is apparent in the fact that one of the stone structures that speaks in Richard Murphy's *The Price of Stone*, the Wellington Testimonial, declares that there is 'no winding stair / Threading my unvermiculated head'.

Sturge Moore's cover design for *The Tower*. Courtesy Special Collections, James Joyce Library, University College Dublin.

Befitting emblems of adversity

Yeats often returned to the idea of his tower as symbol. In 'My House' he presents Thoor Ballylee and its surroundings as 'befitting emblems of adversity'. The tower, he claims, has had two founders, one a violent man-at-arms,

> And I, that after me
> My bodily heirs may find,
> To exalt a lonely mind,
> Befitting emblems of adversity.

The deftly etched last phrase has countless possible applications.

levelled lawns and gravelled ways

This relaxed line from 'Ancestral Houses' conjures a place that stands in contrast to the tower as an emblem of adversity in a poem that explores the idea that an easeful and sophisticated civilization has its roots in violence and conflict, and may taper off into quiescence when the memory and edge of that violence is forgotten:

> O what if levelled lawns and gravelled ways
> Where slippered Contemplation finds his ease
> And Childhood a delight for every sense,
> But take our greatness with our violence?

Lytton Strachey and W.B. Yeats in Ottoline Morrell's London garden.
Photo by Lady Ottoline Morrell © National Portrait Gallery, London.

The levelled lawns and gravelled ways of 'Ancestral Houses' were inspired by Garsington, Ottoline Morrell's manor house near Oxford where she frequently hosted fellow writers.

Yeats enjoyed the 'flowering lawns' both there and at Morrell's London home on Gower Street. Virginia Woolf had a memorable conversation with Yeats at Gower Street.

Woolf told her diary that her own approach to writing seemed 'crude and jaunty' compared to the intricacy of Yeats's

> ... its seriousness, its importance, which wholly engrosses this large active minded, immensely vitalized man. Wherever one cut him, with a little question, he poured, spurted fountains of ideas. And I was impressed by his directness, his terseness. No fluff & dreaminess. Letters he said must be answered. He seemed to live in the centre of an immensely intricate briar bush; from wh. he could issue at any moment; & then withdraw again. And every twig was real to him.

THE LINGERING DEAD

where the blessed dance

This line comes from 'All Souls' Night', the poem in which Yeats summons friends from the dead on a night when the border between the living and the dead is readily traversed.

The heart of the poem is Yeats's entreaty to his one-time lover Florence Farr to return from 'where the blessed dance'. It had been Farr whose perfect voicing of his poetry had tantalized him with the possibility that he would never open a book of verses again. He wrote of her in his memoir *The Trembling of the Veil*: 'She had three great gifts, a tranquil beauty like that of Demeter's image near the British Museum Reading-Room door, and an incomparable sense of rhythm and a beautiful voice, the seeming natural expression of the image.'

She played the poet Aleel in the production of *The Countess Cathleen* at which James Joyce began his lifelong fascination with Yeats's 'Who Goes with Fergus?' Farr and Yeats were briefly lovers, but drifted into what Yeats called 'an enduring friendship that was an enduring exasperation'.

They shared an interest in Gustav Theodor Fechner's *On Life after Death*, in which the German philosopher posited that 'if you think of a dead person earnestly and intensely ... the dead person himself will be in your mind immediately'. Yeats's 'All Souls' Night' is an elaboration on that theme.

From her death-bed in Ceylon, Farr sent Yeats a poem that she described as expressing Fechner's 'idea of our being senses &

thoughts' of the dead. Her poem is a tribute to her stoicism in the face of encroaching death and an expression of her belief that her 'wild ghost' could yet be heard reverberating through time:

> The Earth and We
> We are the eyes, the sense, the vision of Earth
> And she is just a Kerub face that floats
> Dancing and laughing round the sun. In mirth
> She hides in cloaking masks of night and gloats
> In shadows ov'r her aureol of beams
> Like coloured feathers in St. Michael's wings.
> When we are dead she makes thoughts of our dreams;
> And if we are remembered when she sings
> Her song to the sun; 'tis because our wild ghosts
> Clamour within her, till she suddenly screams
> Tragic notes – wakening tremendous strings
> Reverberating, calling Fame's starry hosts.

This is the background to Yeats's summoning Farr's spirit in 'All Souls' Night', recounting how

> ... she ravelled out
> From a discourse in figurative speech
> By some learned Indian
> On the soul's journey. How it is whirled about,
> Wherever the orbit of the moon can reach,
> Until it plunge into the sun;
> And there, free and yet fast,
> Being both Chance and Choice,
> Forget its broken toys
> And sink into its own delight at last.

Friendship never ends: Florence Farr in a publicity photo for *A Sicilian Idyll*.
Courtesy Senate House Library, University of London.

It is no surprise that the author of 'All Souls' Night' admired Lafcadio Hearn's comment that 'there is something ghostly in all great art'. Yeats turned Hearn's observation into a definition of poetry, saying, 'If ever you want a definition of poetry there has been none, not in this last four hundred years, as short and to the point as [Gavin Douglass's] "pleasance and half wonder", though sometimes I prefer the full wonder of Lafcadio Hearn's "there is something ghostly in all great art".'

Hearn was fascinated by ghosts throughout a peripatetic life that began on Lefkada in the Ionian Sea. As he told Yeats in a letter, his childhood in Ireland was imbued with 'fairy-tales and ghost-stories', and his love for these 'Irish things' prompted his 'violent protest' against Yeats's revisions to 'The Host of the Air'. The revised version retained the original's account of a bride's abduction by fairies, but eliminated lines about the husband returning home to find mourners keening his dead bride – a change that, Hearn wrote, 'tore the heart out of it'.

Hearn complained that the original version was a 'wonderful thing' but that Yeats had 'mangled it, maimed it, deformed it, extenuated it – destroyed it totally ... You have really sinned a great sin!' Hearn's vehemence bespeaks the strength of his conviction that Yeats's first version had perfectly expressed an important truth about the interaction between the material and spiritual worlds. Hearn was a reader who believed in the power of a poet's words.

Hearn spent his last fourteen years in Japan, where he taught at the Imperial University and identified elements of Japanese thought that parallel the ideas of Yeats and Farr about the role of the dead among the living. Immersed in Japanese culture, he believed that the ethics of Shinto resulted in the dead exercising a guiding influence over the living. 'The dead move us;' he wrote, 'their ghostly fingers stir the strings of every life in this world's incomprehensible puppet show.'

the nearness of the dead to the living

The idea that we are inhabited by the thoughts of the dead was but one instance of Yeats's general belief in what he described in an essay as the central message of Irish folklore: 'the nearness of the dead to the living'.

Yeats's praise for Joyce's *Dubliners* may be related to the fact that its signature story 'The Dead' is suffused with the nearness of the dead to the living.

In Joyce's story, the dead Michael Furey, who had courted Gretta Conroy in her youth, suddenly looms over her marriage when she hears the song he used to sing to her, 'The Lass of Aughrim'. Her husband Gabriel's sense of himself is shaken by her answer to his query as to the cause of Michael Furey's death: 'I think he died for me.' As Gabriel digests Gretta's troubling answer, Joyce concludes the story with an explicit reminder of the lingering presence of the dead:

> Yes, the newspapers were right: snow was general all over Ireland. It was falling on every part of the dark central plane, on the treeless hills, falling softly upon the Bog of Allen and, farther westward, softly falling into the dark mutinous Shannon waves. It was falling, too, upon every part of the lonely churchyard on the hill where Michael Furey lay buried. It lay thickly drifted on the crooked crosses and headstones, on the spears of the little gate, on the barren thorns. His soul swooned slowly as he heard the snow falling faintly through the universe and faintly falling, like the descent of their last end, upon all the living and the dead.

One needn't be a literalist of the imagination to feel the power of these reminders of the proximity of the dead to the living.

Elizabeth Bowen poignantly pictured the lingering dead in *The Heat of the Day*, where London's World War II bombing victims

> made their anonymous presence – not as today's dead but as yesterday's living – felt through London. Uncounted, they continued to move in shoals through the city day, pervading everything to be seen or heard or felt with their torn-off senses, drawing on this tomorrow they had expected – for death cannot be so sudden as all that … The wall between the living and the dead thinned.

Yeats grounded his notion of the nearness of the dead in his strong sense of place. He wrote that the passionate dead return to the places to which they were attached during life. In particular, he says, 'the shadows of the famous dead come to our elbow amid their old undisturbed habitations'. In such places, 'they tread the corridor and take the empty chair'.

While waiting for Godot, Beckett's Estragon and Vladimir have their own mordant take on the nearness of the dead:

> Estragon
> All the dead voices. …
> Vladimir
> What do they say?
> Estragon
> They talk about their lives.
> Vladimir
> To have lived is not enough for them.
> Estragon
> They have to talk about it.

Vladimir
To be dead is not enough for them.
Estragon
It is not sufficient.

A brief parting from those dear
Is the worst man has to fear

The idea that the dead will be re-united with the living is another
way of thinking about the nearness of the dead to the living. Yeats
expressed his adherence to a variant of this idea, the ancient notion
of reincarnation, in his late poem 'Under Ben Bulben':

> Many times man lives and dies
> Between his two eternities,
> That of race and that of soul,
>
> ...
>
> A brief parting from those dear
> Is the worst man has to fear.
> Though grave-diggers' toil is long,
> Sharp their spades, their muscle strong,
> They but thrust their buried men
> Back in the human mind again.

In Virginia Woolf's *To the Lighthouse*, lines of poetry suggesting reincarnation took possession of Mrs Ramsay's mind
when she heard her husband recite them. The words were from
the poem 'Luriana Lurilee' by Charles Elton:

I wonder if it seems to you,
Luriana, Lurilee,
That all the lives we ever lived
And all the lives to be,
are full of trees and changing leaves,
Luriana, Lurilee.

These words had an effect on Mrs Ramsay of the kind to which John Keats alluded in the comment quoted in the Introduction that a poem 'should strike the reader as a wording of his own highest thoughts, and appear almost a remembrance'. Woolf put it this way: 'like music, the words seemed to be spoken by her own voice, outside her self, saying quite easily and naturally what had been in her mind the whole evening while she said different things'.

The words linger in Mrs Ramsay's mind, and later that evening 'words, like little shaded lights, one red, one blue, one yellow, lit up in the dark of her mind, and seemed leaving their perches up there to fly across and across, or to cry out and to be echoed …

And all the lives we ever lived
And all the lives to be,
Are full of trees and changing leaves,

she murmured'.

Elton's lines also brought comfort to Catherine Smyth. In her memoir *All the Lives We Ever Lived*, she thinks of the speaker and his subject in the poem 'living over and over and over again' so that 'nothing gets lost, everything gets carried forward'. She recognizes that it's just a fantasy, but says, 'I can't shake it: to think that Mrs Ramsay's light is burning; to think my father's light is burning; that they survive in me, in you; that even in their absence they will guide us … A fantasy, yes, but its relief and happiness are real.'

She goes about her house erect and calm ...
as though her darling lived,
But for her grandson now

Yeats used this idea of the dead guiding the living in 'Shepherd and Goatherd', one of his efforts to commemorate his friend Lady Gregory's son, Robert, a pilot in the Royal Air Corps in World War I, who was killed when his plane crashed. In the first letter Gregory wrote after Robert's death, she linked him to the continuing life at Coole through his son, Richard. 'Last month', she wrote, 'I was planting for Robert, now I am planting for Richard.' Yeats's multiple efforts to commemorate his friend's son occasioned many memorable lines of poetry.

A lonely impulse of delight

That Robert had no traditional reason to volunteer for service as a pilot is apparent in the words Yeats imaginatively attributes to him in 'An Irish Airman Foresees His Death': 'Those that I fight I do not hate, / Those that I guard I do not love'. Rather, in a line that fits countless mysterious motivations, it was a 'lonely impulse of delight' that drove Gregory to 'this tumult in the clouds'.

In the film *Memphis Belle*, Sgt Danny Daly, a crewman on a World War II aircraft, tries to impress by reciting Yeats's poem as his own.

Some burn damp faggots, others may consume
The entire combustible world in one small room ...
Because the work had finished in that flare

The elegy 'In Memory of Major Robert Gregory' contains these words of consolation for an early death. Yeats contrasts lives that drag on like damp, slow-burning sticks with one that vanishes in a flash because the work had finished in that flare.

What made us dream that he could comb grey hair?

Yeats regularly shows how to communicate by asking a question. Provocative queries dot his poetic landscape. Meditating on the process of learning in 'Among School Children', he asks, 'How can we know the dancer from the dance?' A related question is posed in the very different circumstances of 'Leda and the Swan': 'Did she put on his knowledge with his power?'

In his elegy for Robert Gregory, the question quoted above consoles by challenging our routine assumptions about longevity. Yeats's intriguing question suggests that we should not be surprised by the brevity of a life packed with accomplishment.

that discourtesy of death

Yeats's elegy pictures Robert Gregory as the embodiment of the perfect Renaissance courtier described in Castiglione's *Il Cortegiano*. In his essay 'Poetry and Tradition', written after visiting Urbino, the site of the conversations immortalized in *Il Cortegiano*, Yeats distilled from Castiglione the importance of the 'shaping' power of 'courtesy and self-possession', rooted in 'a continual deliberate self-delighting happiness'. For the courteous Gregory, who had accompanied his mother and Yeats to Urbino, death is a discourtesy. Yeats says of other deceased friends,

> I am accustomed to their lack of breath,
> But not that my dear friend's dear son,
> Our Sidney and our perfect man,
> Could share in that discourtesy of death.

Yeats's words echo in Susan Sontag's reference to the 'indiscretion of illness'.

a thought
Of that late death took all my heart for speech

Grief silences the elegy.

Elizabeth Bishop's elegy for Robert Lowell, 'North Haven', abounds with echoes of 'In Memory of Major Robert Gregory'. The delighted eye, cold Clare rock, and combustible straw of Yeats's elegy reverberate in the delight, the 'rock, / afloat in mystic blue' and the 'Fragrant Bedstraw's incandescent stars' in Bishop's heart-breaking elegy for her great, troubling and troubled friend.

For example, when Bishop tells her absent friend, 'You left North Haven, anchored in its rock,' there is an echo of Yeats's Gregory 'born / To cold Clare rock and Galway rock and thorn'. Bishop's lament that her constantly revising fellow poet 'cannot change' parallels Gregory's truncated development as a painter. Such interruptions in a creative life are enacted in Yeats's elegy when 'a thought / Of that late death took all my heart for speech'.

Cycles

Things fall apart; the centre cannot hold

This line from 'The Second Coming' – written in 1919 – so perfectly captures the zeitgeist of much of the last hundred years that it and related lines are frequently quoted by politicians and journalists. For example, Fintan O'Toole has calculated that 'The centre cannot hold' was tweeted or retweeted 499 times on 24 June 2016, the morning after the shock of the vote of the UK electorate to leave the European Union. O'Toole has suggested that Yeats's 'brilliance lay in his ability to turn … immediate anxieties into words that seem capable of articulating every kind of epic political disturbance'.

Lines from 'The Second Coming' are pressed into service so often that it has been proposed that they be retired. This facile suggestion overlooks the fact that the reason for the popularity of these lines is their enormous power of 'poetic concentration'. They epitomize poetry's ability to compress, as Jane Hirshfield put it, 'great sweeps of thought, emotion, and perception' into 'forms the mind is able to hold – into images, sentences, and stories that serve as entrance tokens to large and often slippery realms of being'. The reason we hear these words so often is that they 'hold fast in the mind, seeded with the surplus of beauty and meaning that is concentration's mark'. They are talismans that open the door to further engagement.

Phrases from 'The Second Coming' are regularly employed by other writers. A well-known example is Chinua Achebe's 1958 novel *Things Fall Apart*, which takes both its title and its epigraph from Yeats's poem.

And what rough beast, its hour come round at last,
Slouches towards Bethlehem to be born?

Yeats was one of those writers Lionel Trilling described, in a different context, as 'repositories of the dialectic of their times' who contain 'both the yes and the no of their culture, and by that token … were prophetic of the future'. War and violence are a part of Yeats's poetry because they were a part of the dialectic of his times, but the violence of 'The Second Coming' is located in the imagination, and poetry itself is intimately involved with violence. Indeed, Wallace Stevens defined the nobility from which poetry arises as 'a violence from within that protects us from violence without … the imagination pressing back against the pressure of reality'.

These concluding lines of 'The Second Coming' explain the poem's depiction of violent chaos in terms of Yeats's theory that history unfolds in recurring cycles rather than in a straight line. He posited an over-arching cycle in which the era beginning in 2000 would be accompanied by an influx of apocalyptic chaos as the antithesis of a gentler influx at Christ's birth, two thousand years earlier. In Stevens's terms, Yeats's poem is an example of how poetry 'creates the world to which we turn incessantly and without knowing it, and … gives to life the supreme fictions without which we are unable to conceive of it'.

Joan Didion famously chose *Slouching Towards Bethlehem* as the title of her 1967 essay that critic Jonathan Yardley called 'a devastating depiction of the aimless lives of the disaffected and incoherent young' in the Haight-Asbury district of San Francisco. In her preface Didion wrote,

> I went to San Francisco because I had not been able to work in some months, had been paralyzed by the conviction that writing was an irrelevant act, that the world as I had understood it no longer existed. If I was to work again at all, it would be necessary for me to come to terms with disorder.

'The Second Coming' provides a framework for finding order in chaos. It reflects what T.R. Henn called Yeats's 'curious clarity of vision which is not a clarity of detail, but rather of imaginative focus; a sense of the processional element in life and in history'.

The historical background of 'The Second Coming', which was written in January 1919, is revealing. World War I and the rise of Bolshevism were among many factors that fuelled the cauldron of emotion out of which the poem arose. As Ambassador Daniel Mulhall has noted, the Spanish flu pandemic, which had inflicted life-threatening illnesses on Yeats's father and wife in November 1918, was also part of the historical background. The emergence of the Covid-19 pandemic exactly a century after Yeats wrote 'The Second Coming' is a tragic example of the tendency of history to recur in cycles.

Yeats's poem speaks to our current predicaments even though it is unlikely he could have foreseen their particulars. Writer and translator Laura Marris's comment on Albert Camus's *The Plague* is an instructive analogy. Characterizing the titular plague as 'a metaphor for war, the creep of fascism, the horror of Vichy France collaborating in mass murder', she suggests that Camus intended his novel to 'be a kind of serum for the future' because he 'knew that his book would be needed again, long after his death, in a context he couldn't predict or imagine'. She grounds her view in the novel's closing admonition that the plague's originating germ of hatred 'never dies or disappears, that it can lie dormant for decades in furniture and linens, that it waits patiently in rooms, in basements, in trunks, among handkerchiefs and paperwork' until one day it returns. Similarly, 'The Second Coming' reflects Yeats's theory that the trauma out of which the poem arose awaits its slouching return in ways impossible to predict.

The poem can also be a call to action to avert history's recurrence. As Derek Mahon commented, the cone-shaped figures called gyres that Yeats used to diagram his cyclic theory are 'really a way of asking questions like "Is there a shape to history?" And "Where do we go from here?"'

Yeats's 1936 poem 'Lapis Lazuli' suggests that the creative imagination can lead the way to building a joyous future on the rubble of history's tragedies:

> All things fall and are built again,
> And those that build them again are gay.

Joyce's Stephen Dedalus defines history as 'a nightmare from which I am trying to awake'. 'The Second Coming' is a wake-up call.

An age is the reversal of an age

This line from 'Parnell's Funeral' is a more general statement of the theory of history's recurring cycles. Yeats expressed the same idea in *A Vision*: 'Each age unwinds the thread another age had wound ... all things dying each other's life, living each other's death.' This is one of many Yeatsian variations on Heraclitus's fragment 62, which Yeats copied into his journal in 1909: 'The immortals are mortal, the mortals immortal, each living the other's death and dying the other's life.'

Many ingenious lovely things are gone

This line from 'Nineteen Hundred and Nineteen' captures something akin to the profound sadness that engulfed Mircea Eliade from 'the feeling of "the past," that simple fact that there have been things that *are* no more'.

Although the poem focuses on the loss of political institutions, it conveys a broader sense of loss, something approaching the *lacrimae rerum* or tears of things that Virgil tells us welled up in Aeneas as he looked at a mural picturing the deaths of his countrymen in the Trojan War.

The rattle of pebbles on the shore

And yet there are consolations, as in 'The Nineteenth Century and After':

> Though the great song return no more
> There's keen delight in what we have:
> The rattle of pebbles on the shore
> Under the receding wave.

What a graphic way to describe delight in what we have. Yeats included a draft of this poem in a letter to Olivia Shakespear in which he said that, having recently read Browning and William Morris, he feared 'that the world's last great poetical period is over'. It wasn't.

The last line gave rise to the title of a memoir by James Joyce's friend C.P. Curran, the model for many aspects of Joyce's character Gabriel Conroy in 'The Dead'. Curran took the famous photograph of the 22-year-old Joyce shortly before the future author of *Ulysses* commenced his self-imposed exile from Dublin in 1904.

Asked what he was thinking when Curran took the photograph, Joyce replied, 'I was wondering would he lend me five shillings.' Before leaving for Paris with Nora, Joyce unleashed a flurry of requests for help. He asked Yeats to return his translations of two Gerhart Hauptmann plays that Yeats had been considering for possible use by the Abbey Theatre, and for financial help. Yeats promptly returned the translations. In no position to be a lender rather than a borrower himself, Yeats wrote, 'I am very sorry I cannot help you with money. I did my best to get you work as you know, but that is all I can do for you.' He had already helped Joyce get established as a writer and continued to do so. Twenty-eight years after Joyce left Dublin, he wrote to Yeats, 'It is now thirty years since you first held out to me your helping hand.'

Lady Gregory answered Joyce's plea by telegraphing £5 'with all good wishes'. Joyce, too, found shelter in the house of Gregory's friendship.

James Joyce as photographed by C.P. Curran in 1904.

Inventing and Reinventing the Self

By the help of an image
I call to my own opposite, summon all
That I have handled least, least looked upon

These lines from the 1916 poem 'Ego Dominus Tuus' reflect Yeats's desire to re-make himself into the opposite of the wandering, dejected and unsuccessful suitor of Maud Gonne. The title consists of the words ('I am your master') that the Lord of Love spoke to Dante at the outset of his pursuit of Beatrice, the 'apple on the bough / Most out of reach', as Yeats describes her.

Yeats pictures a poet dwelling in an 'old wind-beaten tower' meditating about Dante and Keats, poets who remade themselves through their art. At the close of the poem, the tower-dwelling poet summons his domineering anti-self:

> I call to the mysterious one who yet
> Shall walk the wet sands by the edge of the stream
> And look most like me, being indeed my double,
> And prove of all imaginable things
> The most unlike, being my anti-self ...

These lines reflect Yeats's belief, influenced by Walter Pater and Oscar Wilde, that life is a performance. He made these ideas his own, proclaiming that, 'Active virtue, as distinguished from the passive acceptance of a current code is ... theatrical, consciously dramatic, the wearing of a mask.' For Yeats, performance of an imagined self was 'the condition of arduous full life'.

Yeats's wrestling with his anti-self gave rise to his arresting observation, 'We begin to live when we have conceived life as tragedy.' The idea of life as a performance appeals to Irish writers. George Bernard Shaw gave simple expression to this idea when he advised BBC listeners, 'Life isn't about finding yourself. Life is about creating yourself.'

Only the wasteful virtues earn the sun

Yeats's inscription 'only the wasteful virtues earn the sun'. Courtesy Yeats Society, Sligo.

In the prefatory lines to his 1914 volume *Responsibilities*, Yeats addressed his forebearers. 'Pardon, old fathers,' he began, 'if you still remain / Somewhere in ear-shot for the story's end'.

With his fruitless pursuit of Maud Gonne in mind, he specifically sought,

> Pardon that for a barren passion's sake,
> Although I have come close on forty-nine
> I have no child, I have nothing but a book,
> Nothing but that to prove your blood and mine.

One of the several 'old fathers' addressed by name was his mother's father, William Pollexfen, 'silent and fierce old man', whose example taught the young Yeats that 'Only the wasteful virtues earn the sun'. In *Reveries Over Childhood and Youth* Yeats tells us that his grandfather

> had great physical strength and had the reputation of never ordering a man to do anything he would not do himself. He owned many sailing-ships and once, when a captain just come to anchor at Rosses Point reported something wrong with the rudder, had sent a messenger to say, 'Send a man down to find out what's wrong'. 'The crew all refuse', was the answer, and to that my grandfather answered, 'Go down yourself', and not being obeyed, he dived from the main deck, all the neighbourhood lined along the pebbles of the shore. He came up with his skin torn but well-informed about the rudder. He had a violent temper and kept a hatchet at his bedside for burglars …
>
> Even today when I read *King Lear* his image is always before me, and I often wonder if the delight in passionate men in my plays and in my poetry is more than his memory.

Jack B. Yeats, *Memory Harbour*, 1915. © Estate of Jack B. Yeats, DACS London/IVARO Dublin, 2019.

In dreams begins responsibility

Yeats launched this intriguing thought as an epigraph to *Responsibilities*. The line is followed by the puzzling attribution 'OLD PLAY'. No such play has been identified.

Several months after *Responsibilities* was published, Yeats's father wrote a comment about dreams and responsibility in a letter to his son that resonates in our age of information overload:

> In modern life are no dreams, nothing but an overpowering and shining actuality and its logical processes. The dream workshop is deserted and no one visits the oracles – all are out in the crowded streets.

The resulting dearth of dreams threatens responsibility:

> a people who do not dream never attain to inner sincerity, for only in his dreams is a man really himself. Only for his dreams is a man responsible – his actions are what he must do. Actions are a bastard race to which a man has not given his full paternity.

And wisdom is a butterfly
And not a gloomy bird of prey

These lines are from the short poem 'Tom O'Roughly'. Yeats so delighted in the 'Wisdom is a butterfly' aphorism that he frequently inscribed it in book dedications.

He elaborated on the significance of the butterfly in a letter of 26 September 1934 to William Force Stead. 'The Butterfly', he wrote, 'is the main symbol on my ring – the ring I always wear – the other symbol is the hawk. The hawk is the straight road of logic, the butterfly the crooked road of intuition – the hawk pounces, the butterfly flutters.'

Yeats's ring. Its 'main symbol', Yeats wrote, is a butterfly. Courtesy National Library of Ireland.

The ring was designed by Yeats's friend and collaborator Edmund Dulac at about the time of Yeats's marriage to George Hyde-Lees. Yeats wrote to Dulac on 27 February 1918 that the design 'is a most beautiful thing'. Referring to the poem quoted above, he told Dulac, 'I shall have an explanation for the ring ready always, for I have written a poem to explain it.' The ring itself arrived in early May on the day Yeats and George moved into a new house, prompting Yeats to write to Dulac, 'The ring which came for a good omen the very day we got into this house ... is very beautiful and mysterious looking.' George removed the ring upon Yeats's death in 1939.

The butterfly also found its way into the title of a collection of Yeats's plays. Writing to Olivia Shakespear on 2 December 1930 about a projected book of four plays with four introductions to be called *Wheels and Butterflies*, he explained, 'the wheels are the four introductions. Dublin is said to be full of little societies meeting in cellars & garrets so I shall put this rhyme on a fly-leaf "To cellar & garret / A wheel I send / But every butterfly / To a friend".' The book's epigraph followed the letter closely:

> To Garret or Cellar a wheel I send,
> But every butterfly to a friend.

Be secret and exult

When Lady Gregory failed in her efforts to obtain public support for a Dublin gallery to house her nephew Hugh Lane's collection of impressionist paintings, Yeats suggested one of the three weapons Joyce's Stephen Dedalus allowed himself to use in forging the uncreated conscience of his race. Eschewing exile and cunning in 'To a Friend whose Work has come to Nothing', Yeats advised:

> Bred to a harder thing
> Than Triumph, turn away
> And like a laughing string
> Whereon mad fingers play
> Amid a place of stone,
> Be secret and exult,
> Because of all things known
> That is most difficult.

Seamus Heaney borrowed from this poem to say that what a poem 'does is to create a space where, in the words of W.B. Yeats, the spirit can "be secret and exult"'.

cast out remorse

Casting out remorse! Easier said than done. But the benefits for Yeats are both 'The sweetness that all longed for night and day' that he described in 'Meditations in Time of Civil War' and the transcendent experience recounted in 'Vacillation' where, for

> ... twenty minutes more or less
> It seemed, so great my happiness,
> That I was blessed and could bless.

In 'A Dialogue of Self and Soul' he puts the benefits memorably:

> I am content to follow to its source
> Every event in action or in thought;
> Measure the lot; forgive myself the lot!
> When such as I cast out remorse
> So great a sweetness flows into the breast
> We must laugh and we must sing,
> We are blest by everything,
> Everything we look upon is blest.

And I took all the blame out of all sense and reason

Taking blame goes hand in hand with casting out remorse. 'The Cold Heaven' engages so intensely with the central drama of Yeats's life that he achieves an extraordinary vision and poem:

Suddenly I saw the cold and rook-delighting heaven
That seemed as though ice burned and was but the more ice,
And thereupon imagination and heart were driven
So wild that every casual thought of that and this
Vanished, and left but memories, that should be out of season
With the hot blood of youth, of love crossed long ago;
And I took all the blame out of all sense and reason,
Until I cried and trembled and rocked to and fro,
Riddled with light. Ah! When the ghost begins to quicken,
Confusion of the death-bed over, is it sent
Out naked on the roads, as the books say, and stricken
By the injustice of the skies for punishment?

When Maud Gonne asked what this poem meant, Yeats told her it was an attempt to describe the feelings aroused by the cold and detachably beautiful winter sky – a sense that he was alone and responsible in that loneliness for all the past mistakes that tortured his peace of mind. The first draft of the poem reflects that it was written in a railway carriage. Deirdre Toomey makes the case that Yeats was *en route* to Norwich in East Anglia near the biggest rookery in Europe at Buckenham Carr Woods.

The energy of this intensely felt poem still reverberated more than three-quarters of a century after Yeats wrote it. As Seamus Heaney recounted, 'gleams of unextinguished thought from that poem broke into' his mind as inspiration for the opening poem of 'Lightenings', which flares into being with the words 'Shifting brilliancies' – winter light in a doorway where 'the particular judgment might be set'. The opening word 'Shifting' echoes Yeats's name for one of the states of the soul after death, 'the Shiftings', a stage in which 'the Spirit is purified of good and evil'.

These echoes are the kind of reverberation that illustrate the wisdom of George Steiner's observation, 'The best readings of art are art.'

The cold and rook-delighting heaven beneath which Yeats composed 'The Cold Heaven'. David Tipling photo library/Alamy stock photo.

All life weighed in the scales of my own life seems to me a preparation for something that never happens

As Beckett suggests in *Waiting for Godot*, it is in the nature of time that we seem to await something that never happens. Carlo Rovelli puts it this way:

> [W]e are time. We are this space, this clearing opened by the traces of memory inside the connections between our neurons. We are memory. We are nostalgia. We are longing for a future that will not come. The clearing that is opened up in this way, by memory and by anticipation, is time: a source of anguish sometimes, but in the end a tremendous gift.

William Empson wrote of the 'feeling that life is essentially inadequate to the human spirit, and yet that a good life must avoid saying so'. Yeats didn't hesitate to say so. At the end of his *Reveries Over Childhood and Youth*, he wrote:

> when I think of all the books I have read, and of the wise words I have heard spoken, and of the anxiety I have given to parents and grandparents, and of the hopes that I have had, all life weighed in the scales of my own life seems to me a preparation for something that never happens.

Irish poets, learn your trade,
Sing whatever is well made

These simple words help explain why Ireland's relatively small population contains such a multitude of poets. Yeats encouraged his countrymen to express themselves in poetry simply by being, as Seamus Heaney put it, 'the pre-eminent theorist, visionary and exemplar of a literature based on the category of nationality'.

Heaney explains why nationality was so fruitful a category for Yeats in terms of Yeats's assertion in 'Ancestral Houses' that

> ... Homer had not sung
> Had he not found it certain beyond dreams
> That out of life's own self-delight had sprung
> The abounding glittering jet;

It possessed 'something of the same resource that the unconscious possessed for Jung, and seemed to promise access to the "abounding glittering jet" of life lived spontaneously and certainly within its own free terms'.

The abounding glittering jet of Yeats's creativity is a source of inspiration for his poetic successors, whatever their nationality. As Heaney wrote in a letter, 'every time you part the drapes and enter that inner chamber of his, you realise you've only been surfacing an external, daylight world, while the real thing has been going on in the poetry sanctum'.

MARRYING

it seemed that our two natures blent
Into a sphere from youthful sympathy,
Or else, to alter Plato's parable,
Into the yolk and white of the one shell

These lines deftly transform a powerful metaphor of separation and longing into an image of perfect union. 'Plato's parable' refers to the story in *The Symposium* that humans were originally double beings of both sexes but that Zeus, fearful of the power of such creatures, divided them in two, 'as a cooked egg divided by a hair'. Ever since, each of us has been searching for our missing half.

In 'Among School Children' Yeats remembers a transcendent moment with Maud Gonne when Plato's parable was reversed and his painful longing for Gonne was healed by a blending of their separate natures into 'the yolk and white of the one shell'. These were not just abstract philosophical ideas for Yeats and Gonne. For example, she wrote him on 26 July 1908 about a dream in which 'You had taken the form I think of a great serpent, but I am not quite sure ... We melted into one another till we formed only *one being, a being greater than ourselves* who felt & knew all with double intensity.'

Yeats and Gonne had discussed a union modelled on Nicholas and Pernella Flamel, a fourteenth-century couple devoted to mystical studies who were said to have discovered the philosopher's stone and continued to live, according to Waite's *Lives of Alchemystical Philosophers*, 'a philosophic life, sometimes in one country, sometimes in another' long after their apparent deaths.

With or without the mystical overlay, Yeats's alteration of Plato's parable is a moving image of union between lovers.

The hourly kindness, the day's common speech,
The habitual content of each with each

These lines from 'King and No King' capture the simple happiness of a couple in quotidian life. In the poem in which the lines appear, Yeats suggests that his non-adherence to the particular beliefs of Gonne's Catholicism about the afterlife leaves him skeptical as to whether they will find as good a life beyond the grave as they have in the here and now:

> And I that have not your faith, how shall I know
> That in the blinding light beyond the grave
> We'll find so good a thing as that we have lost?
> The hourly kindness, the day's common speech,
> The habitual content of each with each
> When neither soul nor body has been crossed.

And all day long we have found
There's not a thing but love can make
The world a narrow pound

These lines from 'Solomon to Sheba', written shortly after Yeats's marriage to George Hyde-Lees in 1917, are the conclusion reached by Solomon after a day of physical and mental intimacy with

Sheba. The lines suggest that Yeats has found with George, whom he described as 'a student in all my subjects', the kind of mystical marriage he had sought with Gonne. Shortly before their wedding he had written to her, 'I will live for my work & your happiness & when we are dead our names shall be remembered – perhaps we shall become a part of the strange legendary life of this country.'

When oil and wick are burned in one

These lines appear in 'Solomon and the Witch', a poem featuring a witch who becomes a medium, crying out in an unknown voice in the midst of love-making. The poem was written shortly after Yeats was overtaken by 'great gloom' on his honeymoon, feeling he had made a mistake in marrying George, but changed his mind when she seemed to be receiving messages from the spirit world via automatic writing. The startling experience prompted the beautiful metaphor of the real and imagined images becoming a single light 'When oil and wick are burned in one':

> Maybe the bride-bed brings despair,
> For each an imagined image brings
> And finds a real image there;
> Yet the world ends when these two things,
> Though several, are a single light,
> When oil and wick are burned in one;

what now
Can shake more blossom from autumnal chill
Than all my bursting springtime knew.

These three lines from 'The Gift of Harun Al-Rashid' are a compact and generous answer to the question whether the erstwhile courtly love poet, who found inspiration in the unattainability of his subject, would be silenced by marriage. On the contrary, his most-admired volumes of poetry, *The Tower* and *The Winding Stair*, are grounded in his relationship with George and their residence in Thoor Ballylee.

Marriage brought this interesting observation in a letter to George: 'Is not love being idle together & happy in it. Working together & being happy in it is friendship.'

We can't leave the subject without an echo of 'The Song of Wandering Aengus':

> Though I am old with wandering
> Through hollow lands and hilly lands,
> I will find out where she has gone,
> And kiss her lips and take her hands;
> And walk among long dappled grass,
> And pluck till time and times are done
> The silver apples of the moon,
> The golden apples of the sun.

A Prayer for a Child

The soul recovers radical innocence

Yeats's daughter Anne was born about the time he was preparing to move into his tower. Stirred by a portentous storm, he wrote 'A Prayer for my Daughter' in a prophetic state of mind he memorably described as 'excited reverie'. The adjective 'excited' alerts us that this reverie is more than daydreaming. Rather, 'Imagining in excited reverie / That the future years had come', Yeats is engaging in what Robert Graves called the quintessential poetic act of prolepsis – pulling the future into the present. He sees his child's future unfold free of the burden of the debilitating hatred that often marred his own life:

> Considering that, all hatred driven hence,
> The soul recovers radical innocence
> And learns at last that it is self-delighting,
> Self-appeasing, self-affrighting,
> And that its own sweet will is heaven's will;

With a soul thus disposed, his child can 'be happy still', no matter what obstacles arise:

> She can, though every face should scowl
> And every windy quarter howl
> Or every bellows burst, be happy still.

Implicit in the prayer – indeed its dominant note – is a wish for love. Joyce's redoubtable Leopold Bloom states the fundamental contradiction between love and hate in *Ulysses*:

Force, hatred, history, all that. That's not life for men and women, insult and hatred. And everybody knows that it's the very opposite of that that is really life.

   —What? says Alf.

   —Love, says Bloom. I mean the opposite of hatred.

Yeats's prayer for his child – which applies universally – is for love and happiness.

> *walk alone*
> *Through Coole Domaine & visit for my sake*
> *The stony edges of the lake,*
> *Where every year I have counted swans, & cry*
> *That all is well*

These words from an unused draft stanza of 'A Prayer for my Daughter' are part of his advice for an unhappy child.

   In these lines and those that follow Yeats prays that his daughter will go to the place in the walled garden at Coole where Gregory had mounted a statue of Horace's patron Maecenas, cry that 'all is well', and wait for the echo. Its general content – 'all is well' – will be fortified by the wisdom in the words of the poet who so often counted swans on the stony edges of the lake.

WAR AND PEACE

All that delirium of the brave

The long Irish history of violent efforts to achieve independence from England was fertile ground for trying to define the state of mind that caused otherwise peaceful and benevolent psyches to turn violent. In 'September 1913', a lament for the country's failure to realize the dreams of past patriots, Yeats chose the word 'delirium' to characterize their mental state. The poem also used the 'Was it for this?' oratorical device that has been a recurring mode of questioning whether successive Irish governments have lived up to the ideals of the revolutionary generation.

> Was it for this the wild geese spread
> The grey wing upon every tide;
> For this that all that blood was shed,
> For this Edward Fitzgerald died,
> And Robert Emmet and Wolfe Tone,
> All that delirium of the brave?
> Romantic Ireland's dead and gone,
> It's with O'Leary in the grave.

They weighed so lightly what they gave

This aspect of the mental state of youthful warriors contrasts the courage of nationalist heroes of the past with contemporary Dubliners who, in the dejected poet's view, '[b]ut fumble in a greasy till'.

'September 1913' closes with this memorable merging of encomium and lament for a generation epitomized by John O'Leary who died in 1907 after a lifetime devoted to achieving an independent and non-sectarian Ireland:

> They weighed so lightly what they gave.
> But let them be, they're dead and gone,
> They're with O'Leary in the grave.

All changed, changed utterly:
A terrible beauty is born

This haunting refrain concludes the first stanza of 'Easter 1916', an about-face aptly described as a palinode, the Greeks' term for a poem that retracts a predecessor poem. Yeats immediately recognized that the Easter 1916 Rising had changed things utterly, and that a beauty was born, but it was a 'terrible' one. Both lines of the refrain so perfectly define the essence of this transformative event that they have taken on lives of their own. The rest of the first stanza is equally memorable, especially the descriptive 'vivid faces' of the rebels, which became the title of Roy Foster's group biography of the revolutionary generation:

> I have met them at close of day
> Coming with vivid faces
> From counter or desk among grey
> Eighteenth-century houses.
> I have passed with a nod of the head
> Or polite meaningless words,
> Or have lingered awhile and said
> Polite meaningless words,
> And thought before I had done
> Of a mocking tale or a gibe
> To please a companion
> Around the fire at the club,
> Being certain that they and I
> But lived where motley is worn:
> All changed, changed utterly:
> A terrible beauty is born.

The rhythmic beat is hypnotic. 'Easter 1916' has been Paula Meehan's favourite Yeats poem ever since, at age eleven, she heard Miss Shannon beat out the metre with her stick at Central Model girls school in Gardiner Street in 1966, the fiftieth anniversary of the Easter Rising. 'They go in deep, these early poems,' she says. 'And this poem goes in deepest of all. Mesmeric and mysterious.'

Too long a sacrifice
Can make a stone of the heart

This simple observation undercuts the destructive blood sacrifice tradition that engendered so much delirium of the brave. Maud Gonne disagreed: 'No, I don't like your poem,' she wrote about 'Easter 1916' on 8 November 1916, insisting that 'you ... know quite well that sacrifice has never yet turned a heart to stone though it has immortalized many & through it alone mankind can rise to God'. Yeats delayed publishing the poem until October 1920, but allowed a private printing of twenty-five copies in 1917.

And what if excess of love
Bewildered them till they died?

The idea that the rebels were bewildered is amplified by the observation in the third section of the poem that

> Hearts with one purpose alone
> Through summer and winter seem
> Enchanted to a stone
> To trouble the living stream.

The subtle differences among delirious, bewildered, and enchanted attest to the care with which Yeats chiselled the words that would define a historic event for generations of readers.

Was it needless death after all?

This question makes room for an alternative reality by challenging all war.

Well aware of his power to transform reality into myth, Yeats would later wonder aloud whether the 1902 play he had written with Gregory, *Cathleen Ni Houlihan*, had prompted needless death in 1916. His late poem 'The Man and the Echo' asks, 'Did that play of mine send out / Certain men the English shot?' Intimations of that question prompted Yeats's questioning approach to the Easter Rising.

In 'Easter 1916' Yeats's memorable questions, combined with the provocative joinder of terrible and beauty, launched a phenomenon akin to what philosopher Paul Ricoeur called 'arrows of futurity' in his essay about a new ethics for Europe.

'The past', Ricoeur wrote, 'is not only what is bygone – that which has taken place and can no longer be changed – it also lives in the memory thanks to arrows of futurity ... The unfulfilled future of the past forms perhaps the richest part of a tradition.'

'Easter 1916' is still shaping assessment of the Rising and its unfulfilled future.

We had fed the heart on fantasies

Yeats witnessed the violence of the Irish Civil War from Thoor Ballylee during the summer of 1922. While writing the sequence of poems published as 'Meditations in Time of Civil War', he made a fascinating comment to his neighbour Lady Gregory about the connection between the poems and the violent circumstances in which they were written. 'Lyric poetry', he said, 'is such a fragile thing it ought to have its roots in history or some personal thing.' In the best-known poem of the sequence, 'The Stare's Nest by my Window', Yeats found a new word to describe the impulse to violence. Delirium and bewildered are replaced by 'fantasies':

> We had fed the heart on fantasies,
> The heart's grown brutal from the fare;
> More substance in our enmities
> Than in our love; O honey-bees,
> Come build in the empty house of the stare.

The wisdom Yeats distilled from the Irish experience applies around the world and seems never to lose its pertinence. Early in his life Yeats had foreseen that his local experience would have global resonance, an idea memorably expressed in his pronouncement, 'One can only reach out to the universe with a gloved hand — that glove is one's nation, the only thing one knows even a little of.'

O honey-bees,
Come build in the empty house of the stare

Yeats emphasized the origin of these lines in a note to the published version of his 1923 Nobel Prize Lecture. He seems almost to have willed the honey-bees into existence as an antidote to the bitterness of war. His account told how, in the midst of the confusion, violence and despair of war, he felt 'an overmastering desire not to grow unhappy or embittered, not to lose all sense of the beauty of nature'.

He went on to relate that a 'stare (our West of Ireland name for a starling) had built in a hole beside my window' and that he 'made … out of the feeling of the moment' the verses that begin below and conclude with the above-quoted plea to the honey-bees:

> The bees build in the crevices
> Of loosening masonry, and there
> The mother birds bring grubs and flies.
> My wall is loosening; honey-bees,
> Come build in the empty house of the stare.
>
> We are closed in, and the key is turned
> On our uncertainty; somewhere
> A man is killed, or a house is burned,
> Yet no clear fact to be discerned:
> Come build in the empty house of the stare.

'Presently,' he reported, 'a strange thing happened. I began to smell honey in places where honey could not be, at the end of a stone passage or at some windy turn of the road'.

Yeats's plea to the honey-bees exemplifies what Seamus Heaney called 'the redress of poetry' – the placing of a 'counter-reality in the scales', and thereby generating the 'redressing effect' of 'a glimpsed alternative, a revelation of potential that is denied or constantly threatened by circumstances'.

Seventy-two years after Yeats's 1923 Nobel Prize Lecture, Seamus Heaney used his own Nobel address to breathe new life into his predecessor's metaphor. Heaney's extensive discussion of 'The Stare's Nest by my Window' noted Yeats's ability to distill the emotions surrounding an experience and preserve them in memorable language. 'Yeats's work', he said, 'does what the necessary poetry always does, which is to touch the base of our sympathetic nature while taking in at the same time the unsympathetic reality of the world to which that nature is constantly exposed'. Commenting on how the form of Yeats's poem solidifies its meaning, Heaney instanced the way in which the trio of forces – 'build', 'house' and 'empty' – is 'held in equilibrium by the triple rhyme of "fantasies" and "enmities" and "honey-bees"'.

The image of Yeats 'closed in' with the 'key ... turned / On our uncertainty' speaks directly to our physical and mental predicament during Covid-19 lockdowns. The poem embodies its author's determination not to be unhappy or bitter or lose all sense of the beauty of nature, and instead summon metaphorical honey-bees to build in the empty house of the stare.

Eavan Boland's 1967 poem 'Yeats in Civil War' beautifully captures Yeats's achievement in a way that highlights its continuing pertinence. The poem addresses Yeats directly, first situating him

closed in by his tower, then describing his miraculous escape via
the creative imagination:

> Somehow you arranged your escape
> Aboard a spirit-ship which every day
> Hoisted sail out of fire and rape,
> And on that ship your mind was stowaway.

After recounting how the wind blew the smell of nonexistent
honey in Yeats's face, Boland's poem concludes:

> ... Whatever we may learn

> You are its sum, struggling to survive —
> A fantasy of honey your reprieve.

The end of art is peace

In his 1901 essay 'Ireland and the Arts', Yeats appropriated a line
from Coventry Patmore to define the poet's goal in terms of the
redress of poetry. The poet, he wrote,

> must make his work a part of his own journey towards beauty
> and truth ... for there is only one perfection and only one search
> for perfection, and it sometimes has the form of the religious life
> and sometimes of the artistic life; and I do not think these lives
> differ in their wages, for 'The end of art is peace.'

Seamus Heaney's adoption of this same phrase in 'The Harvest
Bow' is another reminder of the recurring power of a poet's words
to give memorable expression to an important idea.

LEARNING

Plato thought nature but a spume that plays
Upon a ghostly paradigm of things

This graphic summary of the dominant idea of Western philosophy is casually tossed off by a 'sixty-year-old smiling public man' walking, as the title of the poem puts it, 'Among School Children'. Tellingly, he walks 'through the long schoolroom questioning'. With the violence of rebellion and war behind him, this visit to a school is an occasion for the poet to question what he has learned and, indeed, whether it is possible to know anything with certainty.

He starts his inquiry with Plato, who posited a world of ideas outside the world we perceive with our senses. Carlo Rovelli suggests that it was in order to escape anxiety about time that Plato imagined a world of ideas.

'Spume', the word for the foam that flits above the ocean's waves, perfectly expresses Plato's idea of the relationship of things on earth to their archetypes in the world of pure form.

If Alfred North Whitehead was right that European philosophy consists of a 'series of footnotes to Plato', Yeats has compressed the essence of European philosophy into two lines.

World-famous golden-thighed Pythagoras
Fingered upon a fiddle-stick or strings
What a star sang and careless Muses heard

This sharply etched portrait of the enigmatic philosopher who thought that number was the ultimate reality is illuminated by Thomas Taylor's translation of Iamblichus's *Life of Pythagoras*. He tells us, for example, that Pythagoras exhibited his golden thigh as a sign of his god-like nature, that he alone was able to hear 'the universal harmony and consonance of the spheres, and the stars that are moved through them'. Moreover, by discovering the musical ratios inherent in the sounds, he was able to reproduce them with musical instruments.

Pythagoras's claim to god-like status is bolstered by anthropologist Claude Lévi-Strauss's view that since music 'is the only language with the contradictory attributes of being at once intelligible and untranslatable, the musical creator is a being comparable to the gods, and music itself the supreme mystery of the science of man'.

Yeats simplified the role of Pythagoras in a letter to Olivia Shakespear: 'Pythagoras made some measurements of the intervals between notes on a stretched string.' Yeats's letters often add to the understanding of his poems with what Susan Howe memorably calls 'the telepathy of archives'.

O body swayed to music, O brightening glance,
How can we know the dancer from the dance?

Given the references to Plato and Pythagoras that precede this
tantalizing riddle, we are tempted to approach it in terms of
Plato's distinction between our world of appearances and the
timeless world of pure form. Or perhaps it is a challenge to the
distinction between subject and object, inside and outside, that
the mind imposes on experience. More simply, the riddle enacts
its meaning – or at least one of its possible meanings, namely
that the content of a poem is inseparable from its form. The
many efforts to divine the meaning of these melodious lines are
a reminder of Mallarmé's dictum about poems being made of
words rather than ideas. Listening rather than philosophizing,
Seamus Heaney admired 'the limb-sweetening fullness' of the
last stanza of 'Among School Children'.

> Labour is blossoming or dancing where
> The body is not bruised to pleasure soul,
> Nor beauty born out of its own despair,
> Nor blear-eyed wisdom out of midnight oil.
> O chestnut tree, great-rooted blossomer,
> Are you the leaf, the blossom or the bole?
> O body swayed to music, O brightening glance,
> How can we know the dancer from the dance?

Lauding the Olympians

Beautiful Lofty Things

The 1937 poem of this name was an occasion for the 72-year-old poet to rescue dramatic moments from time's onslaught by painting lasting verbal portraits. Maud Gonne could be memorably dramatic just waiting for a train:

> Maud Gonne at Howth station waiting a train,
> Pallas Athene in that straight back and arrogant head:

That single moment immortalizes her among 'All the Olympians; a thing never known again'.

The same was true of the 'wasteful virtue' manifested in his father's dramatically seizing the stage in the midst of the outburst against *The Playboy of the Western World*:

> My father upon the Abbey stage, before him a raging crowd:
> 'This Land of Saints', and then as the applause died out,
> 'Of plaster Saints'; his beautiful mischievous head thrown back.

These lines both preserve a swashbuckling quote from Yeats's father and remind us of the sometimes tense, but always stimulating, relationship between father and son. That memorable moment at the Abbey stood out against a background of paternal prodigality that left Yeats feeling, 'I had to escape this family drifting, innocent & helpless'.

Escape came in the form of the Joycean weapon of exile. In this case, however, it was the father who went into exile. In 1907, not long after the moment immortalized in 'Beautiful Lofty Things', the 68-year-old John Butler Yeats moved to New York. From that liberating distance he wrote to his son, as Colm Tóibín puts it, 'intelligent and compelling letters about art and life, about poetry and religion, about his own hopes as an artist and his life in the city'. Years earlier, at the turn of the twentieth century, he had completed this portrait of his poet son, 'painted', as he wrote to Lady Gregory, 'as if in full tide of talk'.

Portrait of William Butler Yeats by his father John Butler Yeats (1900).
Photo © National Gallery of Ireland.

The portrait painter died in 1922, shortly before his eighty-third birthday. Yeats wrote to his sister Lily the following day, 'He has died as the Antarctic explorers died, in the midst of his work & the middle of his thought, convinced that he was about to paint as never before.'

John Butler Yeats's last full day on earth, 2 February 1922, was the day on which James Joyce's *Ulysses* was published. The elder Yeats had read episodes of the novel and praised its 'terrible veracity, naked and unashamed'.

Three weeks after his father's death, Yeats paid him a great compliment by inscribing a book of his letters with the comment, 'his interests never grew weary and his last words were "Remember you have promised me a sitting in the morning." He died in his sleep.'

Paul Muldoon's poem 'First Words' playfully lists the first words of John Butler Yeats's other son, the painter Jack Yeats, as 'Don't forget your sitting.'

Courtesy Special Collections, Library, St John's College, Oxford.

Let her finish her dance.
Ah, dancer, ah, sweet dancer!

In 'A Crazed Girl' Yeats declared Margot Ruddock

> A beautiful lofty thing, or a thing
> Heroically lost, heroically found.

She was an aspiring poet and actor who became mentally unbalanced when she went to Majorca to seek Yeats's approval of her poems. As she told it in 'Almost I Tasted Ecstasy', Yeats questioned the punctuation of one of her poems, and she thought '"there should be a comma after fulfilment", and that it meant I must die'. She approached the ocean, but 'could not go into the sea because there was so much in life I loved, then I was so happy at not having to die I danced'.

Yeats's poem 'Sweet Dancer' concludes:

> Let her finish her dance.
> *Ah, dancer, ah, sweet dancer!*

Ruddock recovered, participated in some of Yeats's BBC programmes, and published a collection of poems, *The Lemon Tree*. In his introduction to Ruddock's poems, Yeats observes that, when the origin of a lyric is known, it can gain 'a second beauty, passing as it were out of literature into life'.

Augusta Gregory seated at her great ormolu table,
Her eightieth winter approaching: 'Yesterday he
*   threatened my life.*
I told him that nightly from six to seven I sat at
*   this table,*
The blinds drawn up.'

Gregory's fortitude in the midst of surrounding violence was exactly the kind of dramatic gesture Yeats wanted to preserve in the net of words.

We were the last romantics

Several years before writing 'Beautiful Lofty Things' Yeats had celebrated his friendship with Augusta Gregory in this shorthand description of their joint contribution to Irish cultural life. The words, from 'Coole Park and Ballylee, 1931', are so deftly stitched together that they stick to Yeats and Gregory even though they were not part of what is traditionally described as the Romantic Movement. Still, the claim Yeats makes on the basis of subject matter falls within what Joyce Carol Oates describes as the 'romantic striving toward the mythologizing of the commonplace':

> We were the last romantics – chose for theme
> Traditional sanctity and loveliness;

Whatever's written in what poets name
The book of the people; whatever most can bless
The mind of man or elevate a rhyme ...

The poem closes on a note of foreboding:

But all is changed, that high horse riderless,
Though mounted in that saddle Homer rode
Where the swan drifts upon a darkening flood.

Sylvia Plath thought deeply about Yeats's claim. In 'Candles', her own poetic meditation on her infant daughter, Plath revised Yeats's claim, asserting, 'They are the last romantics, these candles' that ignore 'the owner past thirty, no beauty at all'. Meeting Yeats head-on, she challenges the idea that a parent can convey wisdom to an infant: 'How shall I tell anything at all / To this infant still in a birth-drowse?'

Plath's life and work engaged again and again with Yeats. She took the time to visit Thoor Ballylee. Perhaps validating Yeats's belief in the passionate dead returning to places to which they were attached during life, she felt the presence of his spirit.

During the visit, Ted Hughes shook loose and carted away a large quantity of apples, saying, 'When you come to a place like this, you have to violate it.' He later told Richard Murphy, who accompanied him and Plath, that his comment was 'a facetious antithetical inversion of the obvious, in a West Yorkshire style of hyperbole'. He added that he 'regretted not having spoken about the golden apples of the sun, the silver apples of the moon'.

Plath was living in a London flat once occupied by Yeats when she ended her life on 11 February 1963. Her poem 'Words', written within days of her death, hauntingly echoes Yeats's poem

23 Fitzroy Road, London, where W.B. Yeats once lived and Sylvia Plath died.

of the same name and the 'high horse riderless' language that follows Yeats's 'last romantics' claim in 'Coole Park and Ballylee, 1931'. In 'Words', Plath encounters words echoing on the road:

> Words dry and riderless,
> The indefatigable hoof-taps.
> While
> From the bottom of the pool, fixed stars
> Govern a life.

as cold
And passionate as the dawn

Yeats's place in a broadly defined Romantic tradition is firmly fixed by his account in 'The Fisherman' of how he had imagined a Connemara fisherman as his ideal audience,

> The freckled man who goes
> To a grey place on a hill
> In grey Connemara clothes
> At dawn to cast his flies …

Yeats tells how he imagined this ideal fisherman-listener,

> And cried, 'Before I am old
> I shall have written him one
> Poem maybe as cold
> And passionate as the dawn.'

The dramatic conjunction of cold and passion came naturally to Yeats. He wrote in *Reveries Over Childhood and Youth*,
'I persuaded myself that I had a passion for the dawn ... [and]
deliberately reshaped my style, deliberately sought out an impres-
sion as of cold light ... [and] became as emotional as possible but
with an emotion which I described to myself as cold.'

Coldness and passion were so fused in Yeats's mind that,
writing about how tragedy should be a joy to the man who dies, he
said, 'imagination must dance, must be carried beyond feeling into
the aboriginal ice'. Then, questioning whether ice was the correct
word, he answered: 'I once boasted, copying a letter of my father's,
that I would write a poem "as cold and passionate" as the dawn.'

'The Fisherman' spoke to Seamus Heaney in an amazingly
direct and generative way. When Heaney moved to his house on
Strand Road in Dublin in the mid-1970s, his urge to make it 'a
place of writing' coincided with his admiration for two aspects of
Yeats as poet.

First, he saw the possibilities of 'that three-beat pressure-
raising line you find in "middle Yeats" – "Easter 1916", "The
Fisherman", "Men Improve with the Years"'.

At the same time, he became alert 'to the big integration
and vigour in Yeats, the way his affections and disaffections as a
citizen and controversialist could get included and transformed'.
Admiring Yeats's 'marvellous gift for beating the scrap metal of the
day-to-day life into a ringing bell', Heaney recounts that he 'sat
down and deliberately took the hammer to my own scrap and tried
to beat sense and shape out of the loss of friends' in the Northern
Ireland 'Troubles', particularly the eel fisherman Louis O'Neill.

Heaney's comments in *Stepping Stones* give us an extraordinary
view of Yeats figuratively standing over his shoulder as he wrote

'Casualty': 'That was the one time Yeats was an actual tuning fork for a poem I was writing … and I was counting out the metre to keep in step with "The freckled man who goes / To a grey place on a hill / In grey Connemara clothes".'

Yeats's rhythm and his reach for 'the big integration' animate Heaney's elegy for his fisherman friend:

> I tasted freedom with him.
> To get out early, haul
> Steadily off the bottom,
> Dispraise the catch, and smile
> As you find a rhythm
> Working you, slow mile by mile,

GROWING OLD

That is no country for old men

These ear-catching opening words of 'Sailing to Byzantium', which
were adapted by Cormac McCarthy to name a novel, are explained
by some of the ensuing lines:

> An aged man is but a paltry thing,
> A tattered coat upon a stick, unless
> Soul clap its hands and sing, and louder sing
> For every tatter in its mortal dress ...

> And therefore I have sailed the seas and come
> To the holy city of Byzantium.

In the draft of his introduction of the poem for the BBC, Yeats
explained that he 'symbolize[d] the spiritual life by a journey' to
Byzantium. He reasoned, 'When Irishmen were illuminating the
Book of Kells and making the jewelled croziers in the national
Museum, Byzantium was the centre of European civilization and
the source of its spiritual philosophy.'

Yeats draws on his knowledge of Blake's vision of his brother's
soul at death 'ascending and clapping its hands for joy' to picture
his own journey to Byzantium as an intense focus on his poetry,
his soul clapping its hands and singing. History abounds with
instances of writers and artists meeting the approach of death by
even deeper engagement – louder singing in Yeats's terms – with
their creativity.

Yeats's poetry guided the thought and work of Richard Diebenkorn during his last years. He knew the above-quoted lines by heart. In 1990, during a period of severe ill health, he produced six etchings of a coat to illustrate a book of Yeats's poems. He died on 30 March 1993.

The coat as an image of encroaching death reappears in 'The Apparitions', a poem Yeats wrote after a serious illness:

> Fifteen apparitions have I seen;
> The worst a coat upon a coat-hanger.

In Proust's *À la Recherche du Temps Perdu*, the novelist Bergotte, an elderly invalid, makes a risky decision to go to an exhibition because he longs for one last glimpse of Vermeer's *View of Delft*, with its little patch of yellow. Having seen the painting, he suffers a stroke and dies.

In a remarkable series of lectures given to his fellow prisoners as they faced death in a Soviet prison camp, the Polish painter and writer Józef Czapski suggested that Proust, as he wrote this passage, realized that he might be hastening his death by throwing himself intensely into his work in his last months, but that 'death had truly become a matter of indifference to him'.

Samuel Beckett liked to read 'Sailing to Byzantium' aloud, pausing at

> But such a form as Grecian goldsmiths make
> Of hammered gold and gold enamelling
> To keep a drowsy Emperor awake;

stressing the 'm' in form and enamelling, and the 's' with a drowsy 'z' sound, then continuing:

Or set upon a golden bough to sing
To lords and ladies of Byzantium
Of what is past, or passing, or to come.

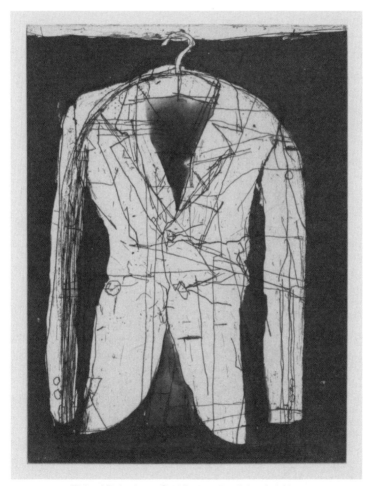

Richard Diebenkorn, *Coat II*, 1990, aquatint and etching
© Richard Diebenkorn Foundation.

Grant me an old man's frenzy
Myself I must remake

In 'An Acre of Grass', set 'Here at life's end', Yeats seeks 'An old man's eagle mind' with which to remake himself through his poetry:

> Grant me an old man's frenzy,
> Myself must I remake
> Till I am Timon and Lear
> Or that William Blake
> Who beat upon the wall
> Till Truth obeyed his call.

Yeats invokes Blake in support of his insistence on re-making himself to the end because Blake had successfully willed himself to renewed creativity. Having written in his Journal of his 'creativity … stopped by a wall', Yeats empathized with Blake, who had written excitedly to William Haley that, upon attending an art exhibit in London, he was 'again enlightened with the light I enjoyed in my youth, and which has for exactly twenty years been closed from me as by a door and by window shutters'.

Yeats's flourishing as death approached reflects his mastery of the third phase of life identified in Seamus Heaney's tripartite advice: 'Getting started, keeping going, getting started again – in art and in life, it seems to me this is the essential rhythm not only of achievement but of survival.'

John Berryman celebrated Yeats's creative sprint to the finish line in his *Dream Songs*. Noting that Yeats 'being old sung / his strongest', Berryman links Yeats with other great artists in terms of what Theodor Adorno called 'late style', in which, as Adorno put it, 'the hand of the master sets free the masses of material that he used to form', leaving visible 'its tears and fissures'. Berryman put it dramatically in this comment about Yeats in 'Dream Song 331':

> he died in full stride, a good way to go,
> making them wonder what's missing,
> a strangeness in the final notes, never to be resolved,
> Beethoven's, Goya's: you had better go to the Prado
> downstairs, to see on what I am insisting.

In the foul rag-and-bone shop of the heart

This stunning description of the source of creativity comes as a shock in the context of a poem such as 'Beautiful Lofty Things'. Yeats's ability to capture the entire dialectic of his time explains why he is so contemporary today.

'The Circus Animals' Desertion' begins with its author telling how he fruitlessly sought a theme 'daily for six weeks or so', then, relentlessly searching for inspiration, concluded,

> I must lie down where all the ladders start
> In the foul rag-and-bone shop of the heart.

The poem describes and enacts the poet's ability to transmute the contents of the foul rag and bone shop of the heart into masterful images:

> Those masterful images because complete
> Grew in pure mind, but out of what began?
> A mound of refuse or the sweepings of a street,
> Old kettles, old bottles, and a broken can,
> Old iron, old bones, old rags, that raving slut
> Who keeps the till. Now that my ladder's gone,
> I must lie down where all the ladders start,
> In the foul rag-and-bone shop of the heart.

Yeats's 'circus animals' were his poems and plays. 'Heart mysteries there', he says of one of his plays, but the phrase has nearly universal application.

Yeats goes on to say that playwriting – 'character isolated by a deed' – was more captivating than the subject-matter of the play:

> And when the Fool and Blind Man stole the bread
> Cuchulain fought the ungovernable sea;
> Heart mysteries there, and yet when all is said
> It was the dream itself enchanted me:
> Character isolated by a deed
> To engross the present and dominate memory.

Yeats's cryptic description of the dramatist's art has equal application to life. Emphasizing that he was writing lives, not histories, Plutarch noted that 'a small thing like a phrase or a jest often makes a greater revelation of a character than battles where thousands die'.

Man can embody truth but he cannot know it

A few weeks before his death, Yeats wrote to Lady Elizabeth Pelham expressing an idea he had long been living:

> I am happy, and I think full of an energy, of an energy I had despaired of. It seems to me that I have found what I wanted. When I try to put it all into a phrase I say, 'Man can embody truth but he cannot know it.' I must embody it in the completion of my life.

Those images that yet
Fresh images beget,
That dolphin-torn, that gong-tormented sea

In a valiant effort to clarify the mysteries of the journey to spiritual life in 'Sailing to Byzantium', Yeats wrote of life at the destination in a sequel entitled 'Byzantium'.

These lines picture the reception of newcomers arriving in Byzantium astride dolphins. The sea is described with a Homeric epithet – not wine-dark as in the *Odyssey*, or scrotumtightening as in Joyce's *Ulysses* – but dolphin-torn and gong-tormented, the latter as much an aural as a visual description.

In 'News for the Delphic Oracle' we glimpse the shore beyond the sea and learn that, 'There all the golden codgers lay', among them two of Yeats's favourite philosophers of the other world, 'Tall Pythagoras' and Plotinus.

One needn't squeeze every morsel of meaning from these words to enjoy the sound and imagined sight of that gong-tormented sea as a proxy for a world outside time, and the image of the golden codgers as an approximation of paradise.

FACING DEATH

Man has created death

Norman O. Brown argues in *Life Against Death* that humans differ from animals not only in consciousness of death but in flight from death as well. For Brown, flight from death is a repression of the death instinct and the spur to human activity. Yeats says it simply in 'Death':

> Nor dread nor hope attend
> A dying animal;
> ...
> Man has created death ...

Implicit in these lines is the idea that, as the creator of death, man can tame it. Yeats admired Jonathan Swift's effort to do so by composing his own epitaph.

Savage indignation there Cannot lacerate his breast

'Swift haunts me;' Yeats wrote in 1931, 'he is always just round the next corner.' Yeats so admired Swift's self-composed epitaph that he called it 'the greatest epitaph in history' and turned it into a poem, 'Swift's Epitaph':

Swift has sailed into his rest;
Savage indignation there
Cannot lacerate his breast.
Imitate him if you dare,
World-besotted traveller; he
Served human liberty.

Swift's attraction for Yeats lay in his 'instinct for what is near and yet hidden', which Yeats thought 'a return to the sources of our power, and therefore a claim made upon the future'. The epitaph's claim on the future is the consoling thought that death opens the door to a place of rest. Yeats quotes the observation of a friend that Swift 'was not afraid of death but of life, of what might happen next'. When Swift's beloved Stella was seriously ill, he prayed that she be preserved from 'all violent desire, whether of life or death'.

O Rocky Voice,
Shall we in that great night rejoice?

In 'The Man and the Echo', written just months before Yeats's death, the man propounds the quoted question in a rocky cleft on the slope of a mountain near Sligo. Because the rocky voice of the echo may be expected to return the speaker's last word, his leading question invites the answer 'Rejoice'. The Echo may thus be expected to proclaim that in that great night that follows death, we shall rejoice.

This answer is not easily won. First, the man's self-scrutiny leaves him in a sleepless state in which he 'would lie down and die'.

The echo picks up these words and suggests that he do just that.

The desperate man is clearly Yeats himself because the acts under examination are drawn from his own life: 'Did that play of mine send out / Certain men the English shot?' 'Did words of mine put too great strain / On that woman's reeling brain?'

The part of Yeats that is ready to lie down and die is vividly evoked. But he pushes back with the assertion that accepting this initial impulse would 'shirk / The spiritual intellect's great work' of standing in judgment on the soul and thereby ordering and purifying it.

Because Yeats hasn't finished this process, the echo has not yet reached his ears, and his distracted state seems ominous. Nonetheless, the word 'rejoice' has been launched and its expected rebound justifies Seamus Heaney's conclusion that the poem manages 'to pronounce a final *Yes*'. Moreover, as Heaney puts it, 'the *Yes* is valuable because we can say of it what Karl Barth said of the enormous *Yes* at the centre of Mozart's music, that it has weight and significance because it overpowers and contains a *No*.'

The man of 'The Man and the Echo' has felt the pull of the urge to lie down and die, but has mastered the art of keeping going.

Cast a cold eye
On life, on death

True to the proleptic description in 'Under Ben Bulben', Yeats's tombstone in Drumcliff churchyard bears this arresting epitaph. The poem writes the epitaph and directs its placement:

> Under bare Ben Bulben's head
> In Drumcliff churchyard Yeats is laid, ...
> By the road an ancient Cross.
> No marble, no conventional phrase;
> On limestone quarried near the spot
> By his command these words are cut:
>> *Cast a cold eye*
>> *On life, on death.*
>> *Horseman, pass by!*

Although the idea of casting a 'cold eye' on life is initially off-putting, the context of its creation shows that it advises a steady, impartial view of life and death. The cold eye was Yeats's reaction while reading an essay stating that Rilke regarded death as 'a goal to be striven for with all the fervor of an inspiring ethical purpose'.

Unmoved by what Susan Sontag later called 'the sex appeal of death', Yeats was repelled by the suggestion of fervid striving for death, and wrote a version of his epitaph in the margin of the essay:

Draw rein; draw breath
Cast a cold eye
On life, on death
Horseman, pass by!

The cold eye reflects Yeats's belief that '[t]he Irish mind has still ... an ancient, cold, explosive, detonating impartiality'. Impartiality requires casting a cold eye on life as well as death.

The impartiality of Yeats's epitaph reflects the hard-won insight captured in a letter to his friend Dorothy Wellesley a year before his death. 'I thought my problem was to face death with gaety [*sic*]', he wrote, 'now I have learned that it is to face life.'

The epitaph catches the eye and ear. Patti Smith created a beautiful photograph of it. Beckett greatly admired it, and applauded Yeats's decision to omit the 'draw rein; draw breath' language when he formalized the wording in 'Under Ben Bulben'. Yeats's son Michael titled his memoir *Cast a Cold Eye*. Larry McMurtry's first novel, the basis for the film *Hud*, was *Horseman, Pass By*.

Seamus Heaney's epitaph, chosen by his family from his poem 'The Gravel Walks', enjoins the reader to 'Walk on air against your better judgement'. Its optimism brings it within the ambit of Heaney's comment on Elizabeth Bishop that she 'continually manages to advance poetry beyond the point where it has been helping us to enjoy life to that even more profoundly verifying point where it helps us also to endure it'.

Yeats's steely command to regard life and death with impartiality is stern by comparison, but it exudes an explosive energy, and is true to its author's belief in the afterlife of the soul through reincarnation. Impartiality follows logically from the question posed in Yeats's 'Tom O'Roughly': 'What's dying but a second wind?'

Seamus Heaney's gravestone. Paul McErlane/Alamy stock photo.

Perhaps Yeats's impartiality *vis-à-vis* his own life and death was grounded in the belief that his life was not about to terminate, but rather to enter a new phase. One sense in which this was true is suggested by the assertion in Auden's elegy that Yeats 'became his admirers' and was 'scattered among a hundred cities'. This is no exaggeration. Witness the extraordinary way he lives on in the poetry of his successors. The phenomenon of Yeats's enduring life resolves the contradiction he posed between perfection of the life and perfection of the work. He is still alive because his work remains vital. He had the magical ability claimed by Robert Graves of forming words into a living organism that continues on its own long after the poet's death.

Seamus Heaney's poems endure in the same way. The third century BC poet Callimachus, librarian at Alexandria, captured this poetic communion in an elegy for his friend Heraclitus in which the voice of the deceased poet can be heard in the nightingale's song. Constantine Trypanis gives us this 'plain prose' translation of Callimachus's elegy in the *Penguin Book of Greek Verse*:

> Someone spoke of your death, Heraclitus, and it moved me to tears, and I remembered how often we put the sun to sleep as we were talking. You, my friend from Helicarnassus, lie somewhere, long long ago gone to dust; but your nightingales are living, and Hades who snatches everything will never lay his hand upon them.

Here is the magic Michael Longley works with the nightingale metaphor:

Sedge-Warblers

Callimachus joins me at your grave
Who shed tears for Heraclitus
And said his poems were nightingales
That death would never lay hands on.
There are no nightingales in Ireland
But sedge-warblers sometimes sing at night
And are mistaken for nightingales,
So death that snatches at everything
Will leave untouched in Bellaghy
Your poems, the sedge-warbler's song.
                    —Michael Longley

But O that I were young again
And held her in my arms!

Although Yeats's widow and publisher placed 'Under Ben Bulben' as the last poem in his *Collected Poems*, the poet himself had intended that the last poem would be 'Politics', which ends with the above-quoted lines. Preceded by a quote from Thomas Mann – 'In our time the destiny of man presents its meaning in political terms' – Yeats's poem insists:

> How can I, that girl standing there,
> My attention fix
> On Roman or on Russian
> Or on Spanish politics?
> Yet here's a travelled man that knows
> What he talks about,
> And there's a politician
> That has both read and thought,
> And maybe what they say is true
> Of war and war's alarms,
> But O that I were young again
> And held her in my arms!

When 'Politics' was moved to the end of a new edition of *Collected Poems* in 1984, Yeats the love poet re-emerged to oversee the conclusion of his work. Seamus Heaney saw it all: 'The coldness and hardness remain,' he noted, 'but we no longer have the poet's sanction for taking this mask as the one he preferred for his final scene. "Politics" now stands as the conclusion and its last lines are: "But O that I were young again / And held her in my arms!".' Heaney masterfully sums up the dramatic change:

> A far cry from 'Cast a cold eye / On life, on death'; equally histrionic, but implying a radically different stance in the face of death. It is as if we were to learn that Sir Walter Raleigh's last words had not been his famous shout to the reluctant executioner – 'What dost thou fear? Strike, man!' – but that instead he had repeated the name of the maid of honor he was rumoured to have seduced in the grounds of Hampton Court Palace years before.

Patti Smith's photo of Yeats's gravestone. Photo © Patti Smith.

LAST WORDS

Cuchulain Comforted

Three weeks before he died, Yeats, awaking from a vivid dream in the middle of the night, dictated a prose draft of a poem that was completed within a week. The dying poet, who identified himself with the mythological figure Cuchulain, signified his optimism about life after death by titling the poem 'Cuchulain Comforted'. Seamus Heaney called it '[o]ne of the greatest ever death-bed utterances'.

In Yeats's dream poem the dead Cuchulain finds himself among shrouds who tell him they are all convicted cowards and that, 'Your life can grow much sweeter if you will / Obey our ancient rule and make a shroud'.

Dreams and a search for knowledge of the state of the soul after death had long been at the centre of Yeats's mental life. After a long conversation with him in 1930, Virginia Woolf wrote in her diary that he spoke of 'dreaming states, & soul states ... as others talk of Beaverbrook & free trade'.

Dante's *Purgatorio* was Yeats's source for the sewing shades and the terza-rima verse form, but Yeats's depiction of Cuchulain's surroundings is startlingly new. As Roy Foster puts it, 'WBY's last poetic vision of the afterlife is not a refuge "where the blessed dance", nor the transforming dolphin-journey to Byzantium, nor even the reunion rehearsed in numerous seance rooms, but a banishment to the company of outcasts.'

Yeats tells us what happens next in the final three lines of the poem:

They sang, but had nor human tunes nor words,
Though all was done in common as before;
They had changed their throats and had the throats of birds.

Perhaps Yeats's shroud anticipates the alternative life of the hammered bird of gold and gold enamelling in 'Sailing to Byzantium':

Or set upon a golden bough to sing
To lords and ladies of Byzantium
Of what is past, or passing, or to come.

Yet, as poet and critic Angela Leighton reminds us, Yeats's birds seem more like the flesh-and-blood 'four and twenty blackbirds' of 'Sing a Song of Sixpence' who survive their baking in a pie so magically that 'When the pie was opened / The birds began to sing'. The 'song of sixpence' was in the forefront of Yeats's mind as he approached death. Discussing the difference between philosophy and poetry in his letter to Elizabeth Pelham about embodying truth in his life, he wrote, 'You can refute Hegel but not the Saint or the song of sixpence'.

Seamus Heaney's praise of Yeats's death-bed utterance all too sadly reminds us of his own, texted to his beloved Marie in Latin: '*Noli timere*' ('Do not be afraid'), words that echo those used by Christ in the Vulgate edition of the New Testament when he tells the synagogue leader Jairus '*Noli timere*' because his daughter is not dead but sleeping.

Dublin embraces Seamus Heaney's last words.
Photo of Maser mural © Peter Higgins @ptmhiggins.

Acknowledgments

There could be no greater gift for the author of a book about W.B. Yeats than the advice and encouragement of Professor Roy Foster, author of the acclaimed and indispensable two-volume biography, *W.B. Yeats: A Life*, published by Oxford University Press. I am deeply grateful to him for his generosity with his time and stimulating ideas.

Heartfelt thanks to Michael Longley for kindly permitting me to quote his moving elegy 'Sedge-Warblers'.

The spirit of the late and beloved Seamus Heaney hovers over this book. His friendship is a lasting treasure.

The Collected Letters of W.B. Yeats, published by Oxford University Press under the general editorship of Professor John Kelly, are essential backdrop to any book about Yeats because of the letters themselves and the incomparably informative and entertaining annotations.

The extraordinary devotion and scholarship of Professor Warwick Gould and Deirdre Toomey make *The Yeats Annual* a rich source of context and depth for all writers about Yeats.

I am grateful to Antony Farrell of Lilliput Press for his commitment to the book and wise counsel, to Ruth Hallinan for expertly overseeing production, and to Marsha Swan of Iota for her exceptional editorial and design contributions to making a beautiful book.

Thanks to Paula Meehan for her close reading and sage advice, to Richard Parrino for his informed and generous editorial guidance, and to Theo Dorgan, Professor James Flannery, Christopher Griffin, David Hensler, George O'Brien and Patrick Welsh for their ideas, support and encouragement.

Thanks to Professor Bon Koizumi of the University of Shimane, great grandson of Lafcadio Hearn, for his courtesy in permitting access to and quotation from Hearn's letters to Yeats; to Professor Akiko Manabe, Shiga University, for her insights into the relationship between Yeats and Hearn; and to Hearn biographer and editor Paul Murray for sharing his expertise.

Thanks to the National Library of Ireland and Director Dr Sandra Collins and Deputy Director Katherine McSharry for many kindnesses, including the photograph of Yeats's ring and permission to publish W.B. Yeats's 16 December 1929 letter to Olivia Shakespear.

Thanks to the John Quinn Papers, Manuscript and Archives Division, The New York Public Library; the Astor, Lenox and Tilden Foundations for access to previously unpublished material; and for the helpful assistance of Tal Nadan and Maurice Klapwald.

Certain poetry by W.B. Yeats appears by permission of United Agents LLP on behalf of Catriona Yeats.

Inexpressible thanks to my wife Carol Melton, son Matthew Melton Hassett, and daughter Meredith Melton Hassett for their advice, support – and everything.

Further Reading

1. BY YEATS

Autobiographies (London: Macmillan, 1995).

A Vision: An Explanation of Life Founded upon the Writings of Giraldus and upon certain Doctrines attributed to Kusta Ben Luka (London: privately printed for subscribers only by T. Werner Laurie, Ltd., 1925).

A Vision (London: Macmillan, 1937).

The Collected Letters of W.B. Yeats: Volume I: 1865–1895, ed. John Kelly and Eric Domville; *Volume II: 1896–1900*, ed. Warwick Gould, John Kelly and Deirdre Toomey; *Volume III: 1901–1904*, *Volume IV: 1905–1907*, and *Volume V: 1908–1910*, ed. John Kelly and Ronald Schuchard (Oxford: Clarendon Press, 1986, 1997, 1994, 2005, 2018).

The Collected Letters of W.B. Yeats, gen. ed. John Kelly, Oxford UP (InteLex Electronic Edition) 2002.

Essays and Introductions (London and New York: Macmillan, 1961).

The Letters of W.B. Yeats, ed. Allan Wade (London, Rupert Hart-Davis, 1954; New York: Macmillan, 1955).

Memoirs: Autobiography – First Draft: Journal, transcribed and
    edited by Denis Donoghue (London: Macmillan, 1972; New
    York: Macmillan, 1973).

Mythologies, ed. Warwick Gould and Deirdre Toomey (Basingstoke:
    Palgrave MacMillan, 2005).

The Variorum Edition of the Poems of W.B. Yeats, ed. Peter Allt and
    Russell K. Alspach (New York: Macmillan, 1957). Capitalization
    of poem titles throughout follows this edition.

The Variorum Edition of the Plays of W.B. Yeats, ed. Russell K. Alspach,
    assisted by Catherine C. Alspach (New York: Macmillan, 1966).

II. ABOUT YEATS

Ellmann, Richard, *W.B. Yeats: The Man and the Masks* (New York:
    Norton, 1978).

Foster, R.F., *W.B. Yeats: A Life, I: The Apprentice Mage* (Oxford
    and New York: OUP, 1997).

Foster, R.F., *W.B. Yeats: A Life, II: The Arch-Poet* (Oxford and New
    York: OUP, 2003).

Hassett, Joseph M., *W.B. Yeats and the Muses* (Oxford: OUP, 2010).

Heaney, Seamus, 'A New and Surprising Yeats', *The New York
    Times Book Review*, 18 March 1984.

Heaney, Seamus, 'Sixth Sense, Seventh Heaven' in Brendan
    Barrington (ed.), *The Dublin Review Reader* (Dublin: Dublin
    Review Books, 2007).

Heaney, Seamus, 'William Butler Yeats' in Seamus Deane (gen.
    ed.), *The Field Day Anthology of Irish Writing* (Derry: Field Day
    Publications, 1991).

Henn, T.R., *The Lonely Tower*, 2nd edn (London: Methuen, 1965).

Mahon, Derek, 'Yeats and the Lights of Dublin', *Selected Prose*
    (Loughcrew: Gallery Press, 2012).

Meehan, Paula, 'My Favourite W.B. Yeats Poem', *The Irish Times*, 10 June 2015.

O'Toole, Fintan, ' "Yeats Test" Criteria Reveal we are Doomed', *The Irish Times*, 28 July 2018.

Toomey, Deirdre, 'The Cold Heaven', *Yeats Annual* 13 (Cambridge: Open Book Publishers, 2013).

Vendler, Helen, *Our Secret Discipline: Yeats and Lyric Form* (Cambridge: Harvard UP, 2007).

Yeats, John Butler, *Letters to his son W.B. Yeats and Others 1869–1922*, edited with a memoir by Joseph Hone (London: Faber, 1944).

III. OTHER WORKS

Alexander, Paul, *Rough Magic* (New York: Viking Penguin, 1991).

Atik, Anne, *How It Was* (London: Faber & Faber, 2001).

Carson, Anne, *If Not Winter: Fragments of Sappho* (New York: Alfred A. Knopf, 2002).

Czapski, Jozef, *Lost Time: Lectures on Proust in a Soviet Prison Camp* (New York: New York Review Books Classics, 2018).

Dillon, Brian, *Essayism* (New York: New York Review Books, 2017).

Eliade, Mircea, *Autobiography, vol. 1: 1907–1937, Journey East, Journey West* (Chicago: University of Chicago Press, 1981).

Empson, William, *Some Versions of Pastoral* (London: Chatto & Windus, 1935).

Frost, Robert, 'The Figure a Poem Makes', preface to *Collected Poems* (New York: Henry Holt, 1939).

Graves, Robert, *The White Goddess*, 4th edn (London: Faber and Faber, 1999).

Heaney, Seamus, *The Redress of Poetry* (New York: Farrar, Straus and Giroux, 1995).

Hirshfield, Jane, *Nine Gates* (New York: Harper, 1998).

Jeffares, A. Norman, *A New Commentary on the Poems of W.B. Yeats* (London: Palgrave Macmillan, 1984).

Jeffers, Robinson, *The Collected Poetry of Robinson Jeffers: 1920-1928*, ed. Tim Hunt (Stanford: Stanford UP, 1988).

Leighton, Angela, *Hearing Things* (London: Harvard UP, 2018).

Lerner, Ben, *The Hatred of Poetry* (New York: Farrar, Straus and Giroux, 2016).

Lévi-Strauss, Claude, *The Raw and the Cooked*, trans. John and Doreen Weightman (New York: Harper and Row, 1969).

Livingston, Jane, *The Art of Richard Diebenkorn* (Oakland: University of California Press, 1997).

Mendelsohn, Daniel, 'In Search of Sappho' in *Waiting for the Barbarians* (New York: New York Review Books, 2012).

Nussbaum, Martha, *The Fragility of Goodness* (Cambridge: CUP, 1986).

O'Driscoll, Dennis, *Stepping Stones: Interviews with Seamus Heaney* (London: Faber and Faber, 2008).

Pater, Walter, *The Renaissance* (1873; New York: Modern Library, 1919).

Ricoeur, Paul, 'Reflections on a New Ethos for Europe' in Paul Ricoeur, *The Hermeneutics of Action*, ed. Richard Kearney (London: Sage, 1996).

Rovelli, Carlo, *The Order of Time* (New York: Penguin, 2018).

Russell, George, *The Living Torch*, ed. Monk Gibbon (London: Macmillan, 1937)

Santagata, Marco, *Dante: The Story of His Life* (Cambridge: Harvard UP, 2016).

Smith, Zadie, *Feel Free* (New York: Penguin, 2018).

Stevens, Wallace, 'The Noble Rider and the Sound of Words' in *The Necessary Angel: Essays on Reality and the Imagination* (New York: Vintage, 1951).

Tóibín, Colm, *Mad, Bad, Dangerous to Know: The Fathers of Wilde, Yeats and Joyce* (New York: Scribner, 2018).